Teaching Today's College Students:

Widening the Circle of Success

Angela Provitera McGlynn

Teaching Today's College Students: Widening the Circle of Success

Angela Provitera McGlynn

ISBN-13: 978-1-891859-70-0

© 2007 Atwood Publishing

Madison, WI

www.atwoodpublishing.com

Cover design by TLC Graphics, www.tlcgraphics.com

Library of Congress Cataloging-in-Publication Data

Provitera McGlynn, Angela.

 Teaching today's college students : widening the circle of success / Angela
Provitera McGlynn.

     p. cm.

 Includes bibliographical references and index.

 ISBN 978-1-891859-70-0 (pb)

 1. College teaching. 2. Minorities—Education (Higher) I. Title.

 LB2331.P769 2007

 378.1'2—dc22

                              2007025819

Dedication

This book is dedicated to all the teachers who strive to know their students, to help their students develop as critical thinkers, excellent communicators and writers, and lifelong learners. These are the teachers who recognize that teaching is an art and who have a passion for the practice of that art.

Acknowledgments

Special thanks to a host of people:

Peter Vogt, whose editing skills are remarkable and whose guidance and kindness I appreciate more than he can know

Linda Babler, the publisher for Atwood Publishing, who helped to shape this book and continues to add valuable contributions and insights to the education literature

My colleagues/friends at Mercer County Community College from whom I have learned so much along with my friends who teach at other colleges

Fran Davidson and Debbie Kell for offering their creative insights in the naming of this book

Kim Nugent, whose e-mail correspondences were so very helpful in fleshing out the ideas for this book

JoAnn Affolter, whose encouragement for my writing helped motivate me to pursue this project

My students throughout my teaching career — they have taught me a great deal about teaching and learning

Ann and Joseph Provitera, my parents who have inspired me, loved me with all their hearts, and motivated me to work hard

Minnie Zaharsky, my aunt and Godmother, whose caring and concern for me has been life-long

Bruce McGlynn, my husband who supports my work, is loving and caring beyond my expectations, enriches my life immeasurably, and keeps me laughing

Phyllis Angeloni, my cousin whose confidence in me is unwavering and whose ongoing support I cherish

Randi Scott, my friend who has an endless supply of unconditional love, David Scott who treats us like extended family, Christopher and Katharine Scott who light up my life, the Rosania family, and all my other very close friends — you know who you are...

Table of Contents

CHAPTER FOUR:

Teaching to Promote Active Learning, Student Engagement, and Critical Thinking Skills in Today's College Classroom

INTRODUCTION

A Personal Message from the Author

My grandparents came to this country from Italy at early ages and raised my parents and their many siblings. My father's dad was a barber and my mother's dad was a shoemaker. My grandmothers were what we would now call homemakers. My parents married in 1946 after my father returned from World War II service. My mother was twenty-one years old when she married my twenty-six-year-old dad. Two years later, I was born.

As children of under-educated immigrants, my own parents placed a high value on education for me and were role models of lifelong learning. In a time of mostly stay-at-home moms, my mother forged a career as a book-keeper and later as a credit union treasurer for a major corporation. My father, who as a child worked prior to and after school to add to his family's earnings, became a court stenographer in Washington, D.C., at the ripe old age of eighteen and sent most of his earnings home to New Jersey to support his seven siblings.

Having achieved the milestone in his family of graduating from high school, my dad developed a love of the law while working in the Washington, D.C. courts. So when I was growing up during the 1950s and 1960s, my father attended college and law school while working full time as a lithographer. Ultimately, at the same time I received my master's degree, my dad passed the New Jersey Bar Exam. He then gave up his printing job and started practicing law at fifty years old. People make career changes more readily these days, but in the late 1960s such a move was quite remarkable—especially for a fifty-year-old man.

I share all of this with you to put my college teaching experience into a historical context—because all of us, teachers and students alike, bring to the classroom our identities in terms of gender, race/ethnicity, social class, age, sexual orientation, and everything else that shapes us—including the generation to which we belong. Generational differences are a major focus of this book, in terms of both the challenges of teaching students from different generations in the same classes as well as the generational differences between us as faculty members and the students we teach.

I'm a member of the Baby Boomer generation. I completed my undergraduate degree in 1969 and earned my master's degree in 1971. One month later, just shy of twenty-three years old, I started teaching psychology at Mercer County Community College in West Windsor New Jersey. I taught five classes each semester, which often required four or five different course preparations, and I was very active in college governance. I continued studying toward a Ph.D. in psychology on a part-time basis for several years—although, newly married and lacking the time and money to devote to it, I never completed the degree.

In my late twenties, I managed to complete a two-year, part-time clinical training program, earning a certificate in family therapy from Trinity Counseling Service in Princeton, New Jersey. The year I was finishing that program, I was awarded a National Endowment for the Humanities Mid-Career Fellowship for the doctoral psychology program at Princeton University, where I studied for one year. At the same time, one of my colleagues at Mercer County Community College—Dr. Florence Rhyn Serlin, a Manhattan psychotherapist—asked me if I'd like to co-author a book with her. Neither of us had any experience in trade publishing. But by being in the right place at the right time, we co-authored *Living with Yourself, Living with Others: A Woman's Guide*. Prentice-Hall published the book in 1979. To give you a sense of the dramatic changes in technology between then and now, we typed the book on early-model word processing PCs and sent pieces of the manuscript back and forth for each other's review via snail mail—because Rhyn, as she liked to be called, continued to live in Manhattan for a while before relocating closer to the MCCC.

In those early days of my teaching, my students were not much younger than I, and many of them were my age and older. The college had a program for returning women back then. I ended up teaching these groups of women, who had all their courses scheduled together—*learning communities* in today's parlance. This was an innovative idea at the time, and one that made (and still makes) pedagogical sense. Unfortunately, the acronym that was chosen for this group reflected a lack of consciousness about women's rights: Women Interested in Furthering their Education—the WIFE program!

In my thirty-five years of teaching psychology, I taught in a variety of modes, including large lectures of 220 students, midsize courses of thirty-five to forty students, and smaller seminars of up to twenty students. I also taught about ten different psychology courses over the years. I've taught people much older than myself, including the GI Generation—that is, people who are now in their eighties—and members of the so-called Silent Generation (people who are now between the ages of sixty-one and eighty). (Lumped together, these two groups are often referred to as *traditionalists* in the literature.) I also taught people of my own Baby Boom generation; Generation Xers (people born after 1965 and up to 1981); and, during the latter part of my career, Millennials, born between 1982 and 2002 by most demographers' demarcations. Most of my classes had a mix of generations and were diverse in every other aspect as well.

My faculty colleagues and I often debated about whether college students are, by and large, the same no matter when they come into this world; or instead whether there are generational differences among students that affect their academic performance, their learning styles, and their classroom behaviors. More specifically when it comes to the Millennial students that dominate today's college landscape, we wondered:

- Were these Millennial students qualitatively different from students of the generations they followed?

  or

- Were these new students basically similar to the students of previous generations?

- Were students making ridiculous (not to mention unrealistic) demands on us as teachers with respect to our time and methods?

  or

- Were we failing to make necessary—and understandable—adjustments in terms of technology, pedagogy, and expectations?

- Were students becoming less respectful and less courteous toward us and their classmates?

  or

- Were we just becoming less tolerant of students' behaviors because we were getting older or perhaps teaching beyond our productive years?

- Were students less prepared to do college-level work?

  or

- Were we more critical of students' lack of development with respect to their academic skills?

- Were students who seemed not to be paying strict attention—by not exhibiting what we perceived as necessary classroom behaviors, such as note taking—letting their minds wander?

  or

- Were students using different learning strategies than the ones we ourselves employed as students?

- Were students not doing anything particularly well because they were attempting to do more than one thing at a time?

  or

- Were students multitasking in ways beyond our own capabilities?

These were the questions we bandied about. My strong hunch is that none of them was an either/or dilemma; there was some truth on both sides. These discussions with colleagues, and my experiences teaching students, led me to write this book. I began to explore the research addressing generational differences among students. As I attempted to find answers to the questions posed above, I was drawn into the research dealing with college demographic and enrollment pattern changes already taking place and those projected for the future; the role of technology in the classroom; and what we as college teachers need to do to meet the academic needs of our students —particularly the largest group of students, the so-called Millennials.

This book will help you understand 1) generational and other differences (especially with respect to the Millennials) and 2) how we as teachers can expand our repertoire of pedagogical strategies so we can widen the circle of student persistence and success while maintaining rigorous academic standards. During my many years of college teaching, I was always concerned with helping students—particularly at-risk students—reach their academic goals. Knowing more about who today's students are and how they learn enhances our capabilities as teachers. That's the focus of this book.

In the pages that follow, I address some key issues in higher education. I describe our students, their learning preferences, and the changes we've seen in classroom decorum; how to manage our classes in terms of student behavior; how we as teachers can better engage our students with the course material; and how we can help our students develop critical thinking skills and become information literate (i.e., able to discriminate and evaluate whether sources of information are credible). I also examine how technology has affected today's students.

Chapter 1 is a detailed demographic description of today's college students and the demographic and enrollment projections for the coming years.

With the picture being one of increasing diversity along several dimensions—including race/ethnicity, age, and socioeconomic status—I discuss the challenges we face in higher education, whether we're teachers or administrators, and offer some strategies for meeting those challenges.

Chapter 2 compares generations of students and discusses the difficulties of teaching multiple generations in the same class. How do we as college teachers meet the differing expectations of students from diverse age groups? The Millennials—or the Net Gen, as they've been called—constitute the largest generation of college students to come along since the Baby Boomers. I describe who these students are while recognizing the dangers of generalizing. In describing the historical context in which the Millennials have grown up, I encourage teachers to be more understanding of Millennials' expectations, values, behaviors, and styles of learning. I believe there must be an intersection—a common middle ground—between how these students learn and how we as college instructors teach.

Chapter 3 addresses students' classroom behaviors—specifically, the relatively new and often troublesome ones. How can you prevent disruptive classroom behavior among your students, and how can you respond to it when it does occur? There is a litany of concerns: lateness to class, use of cell phones during class, rude or threatening behaviors, side conversations, lack of engagement in the class and in the course content, lack of motivation and commitment, the issue of academic integrity, classroom conversation "monopolizers," the use of laptops in class not for note taking but for e-mailing/Instant Messaging and game playing—and the list goes on. In this chapter, I offer you practical strategies that are aimed mostly at helping you prevent disruptive behavior in the first place.

Chapter 4 discusses pedagogical strategies you can use to engage your students, motivate them, and foster their critical thinking skills. The chapter focuses on student engagement as the key to retention and degree completion. In this context, I discuss the *learner-centered classroom*—that is, the shift from an emphasis on the teacher "covering" the material to an emphasis on getting students actively involved in the learning process.

I love teaching and I have cherished my students—students of *all* ages and backgrounds. I wrote this book hoping you'll learn more about today's students and *how they learn.* I've tapped my own college teaching experience spanning three and half decades; my research with students; my review of the research literature on the many topics I've covered; and, most importantly, the voices of my students (some 13,000 of them over the years), my esteemed colleagues, and college professors across the United States who have shared with me their wise input.

CHAPTER ONE

Who Are Today's College Students?

*The changing demographics of higher education:
Implications for the college classroom,
retention, and degree completion*

How many times have you heard recently that the world is changing? If you're in academia, this is probably a familiar mantra. Anderson (2003) discusses three trends that are plainly apparent in higher education today. First, as the children of the Baby Boomers (i.e., the Millennials—who are also sometimes referred to as the Echo Boomers or the Net Generation) enter college over the next twelve years, the population of traditional-age (eighteen to twenty-two) college students will dramatically increase. Second, the college population will reflect the increasing ethnic/racial diversity of our nation. And third, the number of adults returning to college after some time away will continue to rise.

One thing we can be sure of regarding the demographic picture of today's college students: *There is no "typical" student.* In fact, according to the National Center for Education Statistics (Wirt et al. 2002), three-quarters of college students can be viewed as *nontraditional* because they fall into at least one of the following categories:

- They didn't enroll in college immediately after high school.
- They attend college part time.
- They work full time.
- They are financially independent.
- They have dependents.
- They are single parents.
- They lack a high school diploma.

Hamm (2004) says that about two-thirds of community college students attend part time, compared with only one-quarter of students at four-year institutions. He also found that 54 percent of community college students in the United States work full time. Meanwhile, Wilson (2004) found that more than 45 percent of community college students in the United States are the first in their families to attend college, and that almost 45 percent are at least twenty-five years old. Moreover, Oblinger and Hawkins (2005) tell us that 35 percent of all undergraduates are adult learners —with an average age of 38!

Long story short: The "new" college student of today is very different from the students of bygone times.

The swell of college enrollments

In terms of sheer numbers, college enrollments are mushrooming today. Total college and university enrollment hit a record level of 17.3 million in Fall 2004. That number is expected to increase an additional 12 percent between 2005 and 2014. Despite a downturn in the number of traditional-age students during the late 1980s and early 1990s, total enrollment actually increased during that period. Between 1994 and 2004, the number of full-time students rose 30 percent while the number of part-timers grew 8 percent. If we split out the gender statistics during this same time period, the number of men enrolled in college rose 16 percent and the number of women 25 percent (Snyder et al. 2006). This trend of the faster pace of women's enrollment is expected to continue through 2015.

As Oblinger (2003) points out, enrollment growth at community colleges has outpaced four-year college and university enrollment over the last three decades. She also notes that, in addition to the greater numbers of women entering college, more students are attending college part time than in previous decades—and more of those students are over age twenty-five than ever before.

Even the decline in foreign student enrollment in American colleges —witnessed after the terrorist attacks of September 11, 2001—has been reversed. Institute of International Education survey findings reported in *The New York Times* (Arenson 2006) showed that the number of new international students at American colleges and universities rose 8 percent between the Fall 2005 and Fall 2006 academic semesters.

This increase in college enrollments over the past three and a half decades is projected to continue through 2015, although the rise will be somewhat slower than that of the last decade. *The Condition of Education 2006* (Rooney et al. 2006) states that the numbers of both full- and part-time students, the numbers of students at both two- and four-year institutions, and the numbers of both male and female undergraduates will all reach new highs **every year** from 2006 through 2015! In Spring 2008, the high school graduation rate in the United States will be the highest it has ever been, and these students will be facing the toughest college admissions standards we've seen since the number of Baby Boomers graduating from high school peaked in the mid 1960s.

The population increase we're seeing nationwide—particularly among Hispanics, the fastest-growing minority group in America—is making the U.S. a much more racially and ethnically diverse nation. A featured report of the Pew Research Center, *41.9 Million and Counting: A Statistical View of Hispanics at Mid-Decade* (Hakimzadeh 2006), says the 2005 American Community Survey (ACS) put the Hispanic population at 41.9 million, a 22 percent increase over 2000. Hispanics accounted for half of the total population growth in America from 2000 to 2005. Hispanics in America trace their origins to many different countries. In the 2005 ACS, 64 percent of Hispanics in America reported a Mexican origin. Nine percent of the Hispanic population has origins in Puerto Rico, 4 percent in Cuba, and 3 percent in the Dominican Republic.

These survey data also show that the growth has been driven primarily by an increase in the number of second-generation Hispanics due to their more youthful age structure (relative to the overall population) and high birth rates. There are still pockets of the United States that are very white given that ethnic minorities tend to be concentrated in certain states. Over the last several years, however, minorities have begun spreading out into states that were once not diverse at all.

What do all of these statistics tell us? That a nonwhite majority will emerge in our nation's not-too-distant future.

Age and ethnic/racial diversity

When we add age into the diversity mix, U.S. Census Bureau data show that the diversification of America is occurring unevenly. Census analysis of the under-eighteen sector shows it to be the fastest-growing segment of the population. This is particularly significant to us as college educators, since these are the students in the college pipeline.

Anderson (2003) concludes that since developments of the last decade point to increasing ethnic/racial and age diversity across the nation in the future, our educational system must be prepared to handle the changing face of the student body—particularly in those states where, historically, there have been few minorities. Anderson rightly points out that the success of the economy at all levels—local, state, and national—will depend on higher education's ability to provide access to students whose age, background, socioeconomic status, and race/ethnicity are varied. I will add that the access-to-higher-education question is only one side of the coin. The critical issue will be the challenge for colleges and universities to retain and graduate these new groups of students.

How different this diversity is from the diversity we saw just a few decades ago! Thirty years ago, the majority of college students were white and of traditional college age (eighteen to twenty-two). That has changed and will continue to change. When Anderson's classic report was published in 2003, 28 percent of students were persons of color and Hispanics, and 33 percent of undergraduates were 25 years old or older. As Anderson predicted, these trends are growing stronger.

The three demographic trends I highlighted at the beginning of this chapter present significant challenges in higher education and in the college classroom in particular. In our classrooms, we are seeing—and we will continue to see—large numbers of Millennials, increasing ethnic/racial diversity among our students, and more older adults who come from different generations and who thus tend to see the world differently as a result of their life experiences.

In the *New York Times* article "Swell of Minority Students Is Predicted at Colleges," Jodi Wilgoren (2000) reports data from an Educational Testing Service study predicting that college enrollment would expand by two million students in the next fifteen years. Over the last fifty years, Wilgoren says, our nation has seen a steady climb in overall college enrollment. This increase can be attributed to a rise in the number of U.S. births, additional immigration, and a growing belief that a college degree is an absolute necessity for a good job with a decent salary.

As I reported (McGlynn 2000) in "The Changing Face of the Student Body: The Challenges Before Us"—an article I wrote for *Hispanic Outlook in Higher Education*—the ETS study suggested that 80 percent of the projected growth will come from greater enrollment of minority students. The study analyzed the twenty-year span from 1995 to the projections for 2015. In that time period, the percentage of white students on campus will decrease from 71 percent to 63 percent, while African American students' presence on campus will remain stable at 13 percent. The growth in higher education will result from increases in the percentages of Asian American students (up from 5 percent of the student population in 1995 to 8 percent in 2015) and Hispanic students (up from 11 percent of the student population in 1995 to 15 percent in 2015). National Center for Education Statistics data (Snyder et al. 2006) show that the proportion of American college students who are minorities doubled from 15 percent in 1976 to 30 percent in 2004. The rising numbers of Hispanics, Asians, and Pacific Islanders account for much of that increase.

Although minority college student enrollment is mushrooming, the numbers are a bit deceiving in several respects. For starters, the numbers of African Americans and Hispanic Americans in college will not reflect the eighteen- to twenty-four-year-old African American and Hispanic American populations overall. In fact, the ETS study says, the proportions of African American and Hispanic American college attendees relative to the college-age populations in these groups will actually drop. Moreover, more than half of the overall increase in undergraduate enrollment over the next fifteen years will be concentrated in just five states—states with large Hispanic populations: Arizona, California, Florida, New York, and Texas.

The 2005 data from the American Community Survey suggest that as the American Hispanic population grows numerically, it also spreads geographically. The five states with the largest Hispanic populations in 2005 were, in descending order, California, Texas, Florida, New York, and Illinois. However, the fastest Hispanic growth between 2000 and 2005 occurred in North Dakota, Arkansas, South Carolina, Tennessee, and North Carolina. The ACS noted that in the previous five years, North Dakota had experienced a 62 percent increase in its Hispanic population. Data like these strongly suggest that Hispanics will continue to disperse across the nation.

If we look back at increases in postsecondary education enrollment between 1973 and 1994, the overall number of high school graduates who enrolled in four-year institutions nearly doubled, from 16 percent to 31 percent. Within that same time span, the percentage of both whites and blacks also doubled: The percentage of black students who enrolled in college rose from 13 percent to 25 percent, while the percentage of white students who enrolled in college grew from 16 percent to 33 percent. However, the percentage of Hispanic American students who enrolled in college increased to only 20 percent from 13 percent. Clearly, Hispanic American college enrollment rates were not—and still *are* not—keeping pace with either the Hispanic American population numbers or with the numbers of Latino/a high school graduates. As former President Bill Clinton's Advisory Commission on Educational Excellence for Hispanic Americans (President's Advisory Commission 1996) found, this fastest-growing U.S. minority group is at dramatic educational risk at every level of education, from preschool through graduate school.

The changing U.S. demographic picture— A host of challenges

These changing demographic patterns leave us with many challenging questions that need to be addressed:

- As a society, how can we revamp our educational system in order to provide equal educational opportunities from preschool through secondary education, so that the numbers of minorities admitted to college will reflect the numbers of minorities in the population at large?
- How can we increase minority participation in preschool educational programs—particularly in the Hispanic American community, the numbers lag behind those of other groups?
- How can we improve the quality of education in, and the condition of, our urban schools?
- How can we address the teacher shortages—at all levels of education—that are predicted for the next several decades?
- Particularly in light of teacher shortages, how can we improve the quality of teacher preparation in terms of academics and, especially, multilingualism and multiculturalism?
- How can we improve retention and graduation rates of minorities at the secondary and postsecondary levels?
- How can we ensure that colleges and universities will be hospitable, welcoming, and encouraging to minority students?
- Throughout the educational system, how can we promote the development of critical thinking skills, written and oral communication abilities, and the appreciation of diversity?

These challenges may seem daunting, but there are certainly ways to address them (and the many others) we face as a diverse culture. The multi-faceted solutions require the federal government, state and local governments, the private sector, and the school systems to come together. For the solutions to work, according to the President's Advisory Commission on Educational Excellence for Hispanic Americans (1996, 1), "School systems need to form viable partnerships with students, families, communities, other educational institutions, and government bodies, as well as business and corporate leaders."

The swell in college enrollment has also been noted in the report *Knocking at the College Door: Projections of High School Graduates by State, Income, and Race/Ethnicity*, published by the Western Interstate Commission for Higher Education (WICHE), ACT, and the College Board (2003). In this sixth edition of the report, which covers the period from 1988 to 2018, the project leaders point to a number of significant indicators that will change education at every level.

The report features updated projections about high school graduates for all the member states and for the District of Columbia. It breaks the projections down by family income and the following major groups: American Indian/Alaska Native, Asian/Pacific Islander, black/non-Hispanic, Hispanic, and white/non-Hispanic. In a media release concerning the report, WICHE Executive Director David Longanecker notes: "The data we've gathered on the numbers of children, their racial/ethnic backgrounds, and their socioeconomic levels should be a wake-up call, urging us to look closely at what we're doing well and where we need to do much better in terms of retaining and graduating our young people." WICHE Project Director Cheryl Blanco adds: "As our population changes, the landscape of education, from kindergarten through college, is changing too. The challenges we'll face in providing our students with a good education are many—and they'll vary from state to state and region to region."

Socioeconomic status: Family income

As I mentioned earlier, for the first time the WICHE research looked at family income in addition to student numbers and race/ethnicity. With the enrollment surge this report predicts, colleges and universities need to think not only about accommodating more students, but also—more importantly—about ways to facilitate student success. Knowing that low socioeconomic status generally puts students at academic risk, we need to prepare for the influx of lower-income students so that we can help them graduate from college. The WICHE report underscores what most of us in higher education already know: the importance of a college education in helping one secure a well-paying job. Richard Sawyer, assistant vice president for measurement and statistical research at ACT, tells us: "Those with only a high school diploma earn about half of what those with a four-year college degree earn" (Lash 2004).

Regional and state differences

Here are some of the major findings from the sixth edition of *Knocking at the College Door* (Western Interstate Commission for Higher Education [News Release] 2004):

- The number of high school graduates is projected to peak during the 2008-2009 academic year; 3.2 million students will earn their diplomas that year.
- Following that milestone, there will be a slow but steady decline in the numbers of high school graduates in most parts of the United States.
- The highest percentage of growth will be seen in the West.
- During that same time span, the South will see a 5 percent increase in high school graduates. Conversely, the Midwest will experience a 9 percent decline while the Northeast will see a 2 percent drop.

Interestingly, the report notes that the sizes and faces of our high school graduating classes will vary widely from state to state. The researchers predict that Arizona will see its graduation numbers grow 55 percent between 2001-2002 and 2017-2018; half of those graduates will be minorities. Massachusetts, on the other hand, is projected to see an overall decline of 2 percent in its graduation numbers, with racial/ethnic minorities representing only 24 percent of those graduates.

Director Longanecker cites three major reasons for the shifting enrollment patterns: the number of births in each state, interstate migration, and immigration. California and New York, he notes, have the highest numbers of immigrants. He states further: "Public policy will need to vary from one state to another. If we want to be a nation that leads the world, we simply have to do business differently in the future."

Knocking at the College Door predicts that in the high school graduating class of 2014, only about half of the students will be whites/non-Hispanics; the other half will be racial/ethnic minorities. In line with overall demographic trends, Hispanics are still expected to be the fastest-growing group in the United States, representing more than 20 percent of the 2014 high school graduating class. The percentage of Asian/Pacific Islander students will also increase in that class. Meantime, the percentage of black students will hold steady at current rates while the percentage of white/non-Hispanic students will fall.

The study's then-projections for 2006-2007 say that 16 percent of public high school graduates would come from families earning less than $20,000 a year, and that about the same percentage would come from families earning more than $100,000 per year. The majority of students (68 percent), the study projected at the time, would come from families with annual incomes ranging from $20,000 to $100,000. Again, the report describes regional differences. The West has experienced—and will continue to experience—the highest growth among students from low-income families, while the Northeast will experience the most growth among students from higher-income families.

The questions, challenges, and tasks facing higher education

Given what the *Knocking at the College Door* report depicts, what are the questions, challenges, and tasks facing institutions of higher education? In terms of planning, we need to be aware of the regional and state distinctions with respect to growth. Where there are substantial increases in potential college enrollments, will there be enough seats and space to accommodate the influx? When students get to college, will they have been properly prepared to do college-level work? ACT's Sawyer says that we as educators must better prepare lower-income and minority students in particular (Lash 2004). I believe colleges can certainly do more than they are now to facilitate student success. But this report is a wake-up call to public elementary and secondary schools as well: Obviously, the better students are educated in elementary and secondary school, the greater their likelihood of success in college.

One of our concerns has to be the low retention and college graduation rates of Hispanics. According to Richard Fry (2002), although Hispanics enroll in college at almost the same rate as non-Latino/a students, they often bring special circumstances and challenges to their college experience. Fry tells us that Hispanic students are less likely to attend college full time, and that part-time enrollment is an "at-risk" indicator for any college student. Additionally, Hispanics are more likely to work during college so that they can provide financial support to family dependents or contribute to the family earning pot if they still live at home. Latinas face additional obstacles to their degree completion in that many traditional Hispanic families rely on their daughters for home and sibling care and expect them to marry and have children at early ages.

Fry stresses that Hispanic students need special help in balancing their academic lives with their work and family lives. He suggests that community colleges especially—where most Hispanics start their studies—need to improve their tutorial and developmental programs and services.

As I reported in *Hispanic Outlook in Higher Education* (McGlynn 2004a), T. Jaime Chahin—a scholar at the Tomas Rivera Center at Trinity University in San Antonio, and a professor at Southwest Texas State University in San Marcos—says: "Hispanics should feel that college is not a novelty but is something that is expected, even for first-generation students who have never been exposed to these kinds of opportunities" (35). He says that some schools, especially in the Southwest, are making progress integrating Hispanics and their culture into campus life. He suggests that academia needs to do a better job of recruiting and retaining Latino/a faculty who can serve as role models for Hispanic undergraduates. And the process of enhancing Hispanics' academic success, he adds, should begin at the elementary school level. In my mind, this is a message that cannot be overstated. In fact, preschool is undoubtedly the place to begin!

Knocking at the College Door documents some of what we already knew and then gives us a glimpse into future trends and issues that we need to address as a nation. If Hispanics, blacks, and Native Americans continue to be less likely to earn a college degree—and given that we now know the role of socioeconomic status in lack of academic success—it will have been a failure of our nation on many fronts. Such a failure undermines the foundations of a free and supposedly just society, and it certainly interferes with our capacity to build a competitive work force in a world that is becoming increasingly global. It also raises serious doubts about the American educational system's capacity to manage and respond effectively to projected demographic changes.

Young black men from lower-income families

One at-risk group of people who are of striking significance in our society are black males from lower-income families. In my *Hispanic Outlook in Higher Education* article "The Worsening Plight of Black Men" (McGlynn 2006b), I discuss the bleak picture portrayed by several recent articles and books. I note that the common unemployment and education statistics underestimate the plight of young black males in America. The situation for black males has actually worsened in recent years despite the gains made by black females and members of other minority groups. *The New York Times* (Eckholm 2006) reports that experts at Columbia University, Princeton University, Harvard University, and other institutions concur that the large numbers of poorly educated black men are becoming more and more disconnected from mainstream society. Black males are faring far worse than are poorly educated white or Hispanic men or black women.

Analyzing the life patterns of young black men, new reports paint an even bleaker picture of the challenges they face. Ronald B. Mincy, professor of social policy and social work practices at Columbia University and editor of *Black Males Left Behind* (Urban Institute Press 2006), says: "There's something very different happening with young black men, and it's something we can no longer ignore" (Eckholm 2006, A1). Despite the gains made by black women, thanks to a healthy economy and public policy, Mincy notes, young black men have fallen further behind. In fact, black men continue to have a poorer chance for a good life (a decent existence with adequate income) than any other group in our society. Among the host of problems resulting from joblessness and low wages within the undereducated, young-adult black male population are fewer marriages and increases in nonmarital child births.

During the 1990s, the employment rate of sixteen- to twenty-four-year-old black men with a high school education or less fell from its peak during the economic expansion of the 1980s. Additionally, their participation in the labor force continued to fall through the 1980s, the 1990s, and into this century. This decrease in the presence of black men in the labor force coincides with the rapid growth in the number of young black men who are incarcerated or on parole or probation.

In 2000, 65 percent of black male high school dropouts in their twenties were jobless. This statistic includes only those men who were unable to find work; it does not include those who weren't seeking work or those who were incarcerated. The jobless rate of young black men seems to be on a relentless climb. By 2004, their jobless rate reached 72 percent. Compare these numbers with joblessness among young white male high school dropouts (34 percent) and young Hispanic male dropouts (19 percent). When you add high school graduates into the mix, you still find that half of young black men in their twenties were jobless in 2004—and that was a 4 percentage-point increase over 2000.

The analysis of incarceration rates of young black males is just as disheartening. The rates climbed during the 1990s, and they have reached historic highs in the past several years. Note that in 1995, 16 percent of black men in their twenties who hadn't attended college were in jail or prison. By

2004, that number had climbed to 21 percent. Among men in their mid thirties, 60 percent of blacks who had dropped out of high school had spent at least some time in prison.

Inner cities have the worst rates of joblessness, incarceration, and high school completion. More than half of all black men in inner cities drop out of high school and many of them end up without jobs or in prison.

Black Males Left Behind presents a broad picture of this group, describing demographic characteristics such as educational attainment, labor force participation, wages, marriage rates, family structure, poverty rates, and geographical concentration. It then compares these demographics with those of men in the white and Hispanic cohorts. Several chapters lay out the problems: unemployment, under-education, a poor labor market, how employers' perceptions of young black males affect their job prospects, and how there was a mismatch between the location of available jobs and young black males' residences in the 1990s. Survey results of young black men attest to their desire for more work opportunities and more job-related training programs.

Fortunately, the report is not simply a litany of dire research findings. Indeed, *Black Males Left Behind* is an important blueprint for policy. Showcasing the research of seventeen leading scholars, the report gives policymakers crucial starting points and references for tackling the multi-faceted, complex problems facing under-educated black men. Among the suggested policy initiatives:

- Increase job placement assistance and other employment services that would lead to higher-paying jobs. Efforts like the successful Job Corps program could be enhanced.

- Improve public policies to increase the earnings and employment of low-income fathers who do not live with their children.

- Create policies for disadvantaged fathers that address low education and employment levels, high divorce rates, high rates of incarceration, and high rates of parenthood outside marriage.

There are about five million black men between the ages of twenty and thirty-nine in America today. Their struggle is certainly a problem that needs to be addressed. Factors that contribute to their situation include (but are not limited to) racism, substandard schools, absent parents—particularly absent fathers—and the decline in the number of blue-collar jobs. Added to these issues are sub-cultural factors such as glorifying swagger over work and glamorizing "big-bucks," flashy consumerism.

In an op-ed piece in *The New York Times*, Patterson (2006) comments on the new research I've discussed here. He suggests that these studies do not pay enough attention to sub-cultural and cultural factors that contribute to the plight of young black men. He notes what sociologists call the "cool-pose culture" of young black men who are lured into hanging out on the street after school, shopping, dressing sharply, engaging in sexual conquests, using recreational drugs, embracing the music and culture of hip-hop, and seeing superstar black male athletes and entertainers as role models.

It is important to note, Patterson says, that this sub-cultural snare for young black youths is not disconnected from mainstream culture, where they receive strong support from the American corporate world as well as from their peers and white counterparts. "Hip-hop, professional basketball, and homeboy fashions are as American as cherry pie," he writes (4.13). Young white males are also into these activities, Patterson says—but they are into them selectively, knowing when it's time to turn off the music and lifestyle and study for exams. He says that for young black males—particularly in inner cities—the hip-hop culture and what it entails is all they think they have and is their only source of pride. Ironically, the connection to this sub-culture is one factor (in a complex web of factors) that keeps them disconnected from the socioeconomic mainstream.

All of these negative trends seem to be associated with poor schooling. Federal data actually underestimate the high school dropout rates among the poor, partly because incarcerated youth are not counted. (See Gary Orfield's *Dropouts in America*, 2004.)

Interestingly, research shows that high school dropout rates for Hispanics are worse than those for blacks (or any other minority group for that matter) but are not associated with nearly as much unemployment or crime. A variety of complicated, interacting factors account for the differences. Of course, improving retention and college degree-completion rates for Hispanics must also be a societal priority. The new reports call for intensive, innovative efforts to give children a better start and a greater chance for school success. These efforts would include extra "high-quality" schooling for poor children as well as various types of support for their parents. Other policy initiatives would call for less automatic incarceration of minor offenders, and for teaching life and job skills to prisoners so they can transition well back into society.

A better start in preschool, grade school, and high school would prepare young people to enter college. We now live a society where higher education is vital to economic success and to assimilating into middle-class culture. Mincy (2006) says that programs to help more lower-income men enter and succeed in college may hold promise, but that he is dismayed at the current lack of such resources.

The Urban Institute—a nonprofit, nonpartisan policy research and educational organization that examines the social, economic, and governance challenges facing America—recently published another related report entitled *Reconnecting Disadvantaged Young Men* (Edelman, Holzer, and Offner 2006). The report asks:

- Why are so many young people disconnected from mainstream society?
- Why is this growing disconnection more common for young men—especially African American men and low-income men —than it is for young women?

Not only do the authors of the report offer analysis of the current trends, they also present numerous policy suggestions for improving the educational and employment prospects of several million young men ages sixteen to twenty-four who have been out of school and work for over a year. The focus is on African American and Hispanic males because young women have made more progress in recent years. The authors focus on three essential areas of policy: education and training, financial incentives to work, and barriers facing non-custodial fathers and former prison inmates. (For a listing of their policy suggestions in each of these areas, see "New Approaches Address Getting Alienated Young Men Back to School or Jobs" [The Urban Institute (News Release) 2006].) You will find a breadth of ideas, ranging from increasing funding for such proven programs as Job Corps, Youth Service Corps, and career academies to boosting the federal minimum wage.)

In reviewing the authors' suggestions, Samuel Halperin—founder and senior fellow of the American Youth Policy Forum—says (2006): "Beyond the grim demographic statistics, there is now a large and growing body of knowledge and expertise about what works to combat this blight on America's soul. ... In this magisterial guidebook for policymakers, the authors have distilled their wisdom into practical suggestions for public policy."

The rise in part-time enrollment and employment among full- and part-time students

Anderson's "Changing U.S. Demographics and American Higher Education" (2003) discusses how American campuses have changed in terms of the ages of their students and the rise in part-time enrollment. In 1970, about 2.4 million of our 8.5 million undergraduates were students who were twenty-five years old or older, Anderson notes. Over the next three decades, he says, the over-twenty-five group grew by 144 percent while the number of students under twenty-five increased by just 45 percent. By the late

1990s, one-third of our undergraduate and graduate students were at least twenty-five, and most of them (71 percent) were undergraduates, Anderson stresses.

The number of part-time students rose by 117 percent during that same time frame, compared with a 51 percent increase in the number of full timers, Anderson notes. Within the over-twenty-five group in 1999, 69 percent were enrolled in college part time. And the National Center for Education Statistics, Anderson points out, predicts that the number of over-twenty-five students will continue to increase on college campuses until at least 2012 (see Gerald and Hussar 2002).

Hansen's classic study on the demographics of college students (1998) found that employment among students has also increased over time. He found that the percentage of sixteen- to twenty-four-year-old, full-time college students who were employed at least part time rose from 36 percent in 1973 to 69 percent during the 1995-1996 academic year. The proportion of students working at least 20 hours a week increased from 17 percent to 37 percent during that same time period.

In the most recent research I found on employment among college students—an article from *U.S. News & World Report* entitled "Get to Work" —Ewers (2002) reported on survey data showing that nearly 80 percent of undergraduates work at least part time. It looks like that trend is bound to continue. The second annual *National Freshman Attitudes Report* produced by higher education consulting firm Noel-Levitz (Noel-Levitz 2007) shows that nearly 58 percent of the 97,000+ first-year students surveyed (in the summer and fall of 2006) plan to work 11 or more hours a week. The trend is particularly pronounced among students attending two-year institutions: A full 45 percent expect to work more than 20 hours a week, the Noel-Levitz study shows. That finding matches up closely with my own experience; whenever I asked my students how many of them were employed, I was always amazed at the overwhelming majority of raised hands.

Lack of preparedness among many of today's college students

If we look at Hansen's (1998) classic work on the indices of student preparedness, the trends he saw from the data back then still hold up. Among his many findings that seem to be relevant to our current concerns about student retention rates:

- Trends in SAT and ACT scores demonstrated that the overall preparation levels of students declined from the mid 1960s to the early 1980s. More recent data show an improvement but still relatively low performance on these tests, both in absolute terms and by international comparison.

- In 1995, America's twelfth-grade students outperformed only two of twenty-one other countries in math and science.

- In Fall 1995, 81 percent of public four-year colleges/universities and virtually all public two-year colleges offered remedial programs. And of all first-time freshmen, 29 percent took at least one remedial course. (The percentages of students taking remedial courses are much higher today.)

- There seems to be a trend toward grade inflation among high school teachers. One of the many potential reasons: Teachers want to help their students compete in an increasingly tough college admissions process. Grade inflation seems to be occurring in higher education as well.

- Most high school seniors spend fewer than six hours a week studying during their last year of high school.

- Public high school teachers report high levels of absenteeism among students.

If we want to improve college retention and completion rates, we need to find ways to address the deficiencies many students bring to college.

Changes in students' attitudes

In addition to lack of preparedness to do college-level work, Hansen uncovered some disturbing trends in students' attitudes. For example, he wrote (1998, 2):

Despite often low levels of preparedness, students tend to be highly confident in their abilities. Whether due to years of grade inflation in high school (and college), misunderstood attempts to bolster children's self-esteem, or society's overall disrespect for the immaterial value of education, many students tend to look at academic accomplishment as just another commodity to be purchased.

Hansen's findings seem to be prescient when we listen to faculty discussions on today's college campuses. I use the word "prescient" because the conversations in academia these days often focus on the student attitude of consumerism in education. Among many of today's students—particularly Millennials—there is an attitude of entitlement: Since I (or, more frequently, my parents) am paying tuition, I deserve good grades and a degree.

Hansen learned that freshmen in college are increasingly overestimating their abilities in virtually all academic disciplines. He also saw a high degree of academic disengagement among the freshmen surveyed. He found that "developing a meaningful philosophy of life" had dropped steadily over the years as an important objective of attending college. He also found a dramatic increase in the number of undergraduates who believe that the chief benefit of a college education is to increase one's earning power.

Achieving and maintaining academic excellence

Now that we've identified the key trends in higher education—more students overall, more diversity among the students in our classes in terms of ethnicity/race, more students who work, a swell in the number of Millennials as well as a mix of generations in our classes, more first-generation and immigrant students, more students from low-income families, more underprepared students—how do we as educators juggle enrollment management, virtual classrooms and distance learning, and the accompanying challenges of the diverse college classroom with what should be the main focus of higher education: producing college graduates who have developed critical thinking skills, written and oral communication skills, appreciation of diversity, aesthetics and cultural values, integrity and ethics, civic-mindedness, and the skill sets necessary to participate in a growing global economy?

Keep in mind that the trick for higher education is to accomplish all of these feats while state and local funding are diminishing in many parts of the nation. Colleges and universities are being asked to become more efficient and cost-effective. They're also being asked—rightfully so—to become more accountable in terms of learning outcomes. As Richard Arnold (2004) suggests, it's essential that all of academia—faculty, administrators, staff, students and their families, and the community—work cooperatively to ensure that academic excellence is achieved and maintained.

So where do we begin?

Retention and degree completion—
the affective dimension

It is my belief that retention and completion-to-degree rates must be foremost in educators' minds. If we don't bring today's diverse college students into the fold of academic success, our nation will be at risk economically. As a society, we must educate our people not only because it will help them improve their lives and because it's the right thing to do, but also because doing so will benefit us all as a country.

Let's start with the specific setting I'm most familiar with—the college classroom—and then examine the role of the institution in ensuring academic excellence and success among students. Given the diversity of our college classrooms—both today and in the immediate future—how can we boost the chances that our students will be successful in our particular courses? I believe we must pay attention to two influences on learning: the *affective* and the *cognitive*.

Starting with the affective dimension of learning—that is, all the evidence we now have that how students *feel* in class and about their learning influences whether they'll be successful—we must create a classroom atmosphere that students see as being safe, welcoming, and inclusive. Students need to feel a sense of belonging in our classes and at their institutions. Retention studies conducted over the last twenty-five years in higher education suggest that one of the most crucial factors in helping students complete their studies is creating an atmosphere of *community* (see Bank, Slavings, and Biddle 1990; Frost 1999-2000; and Padilla 1999).

As I discuss in my book *Successful Beginnings for College Teaching: Engaging Your Students from the First Day* (McGlynn 2001, 56):

> The bottom line for retention seems to have more to do with students' friendships than with their studies. ...Those of us who teach at colleges and universities—particularly commuter institutions—and who are committed to increasing those retention rates recognize that if student friendships are to occur at all, they'll probably occur within the classroom. This makes classroom atmosphere and dynamics critical variables for retention. The challenge to us as faculty goes beyond learning to teach effectively and beyond using multifaceted approaches and strategies. Equally important—in terms of fostering student persistence—is to create an inclusive atmosphere where students from diverse backgrounds feel safe within the classroom environment. Students need to believe that their voices will be heard and valued by their teachers and their peers. Within such a climate, the chances that students will form friendships go up markedly. ... If we want to motivate students to learn our course content and persist to earn a degree, we need to pay attention to more than how we can best present course material. We also need to manage the class dynamics in such a way as to foster bonding among students. Effective teachers create an atmosphere of trust and warmth between

themselves and their students—and they cultivate that same atmosphere among the students themselves.

Also in *Successful Beginnings*, I offer first-day-of-class suggestions on setting the tone for the semester. I describe various icebreakers we can use to help students feel comfortable in class, meet at least a few of their peers, and learn each other's names. Another resource that features new ideas on getting students to interact with one another is the *On Course Workshop* newsletter (see www.oncourseworkshop.com).

One of the icebreakers I find intriguing—although I've never tried it in class—is described in the *On Course Workshop* by Linda Houston, who teaches English at Ohio State University. She asks students in her developmental writing courses to put items they've brought to class (e.g., pens, keys, pictures) into brown lunch bags, which she provides. Each student trades bags with a partner and is asked to write an impression of his or her counterpart based on the items in that student's bag. The students introduce themselves to their partners and read their impressions of one another. The partners then have the opportunity to agree, disagree, or clarify how they see themselves. After the discussion, students revise their impressions of their partners.

Professor Houston even assigns homework: The students are asked to write descriptions of their partners based on all the information they have so far. She says the exercise breaks the ice during the first class meeting and gets students writing, describing, and revising.

Retention and degree completion— the cognitive dimension

Now let's deal with the cognitive aspects of the learning experience, and how we as teachers can improve the chances of students' success.

We can start with *preparing* our students to be successful. In other words, given the diversity of the students we're teaching and the fact that many of them are first-generation students, we can no longer assume that our students know what it takes to do well in college. The more explicit we make our course expectations, both in writing and orally, the better the chances our students will understand those expectations. They need to know what they must *do* to be successful. The clearer our syllabi—and the more we help students understand the syllabus for each particular course—the more likely even underprepared students will know what *they must do*.

Here again, times have changed. We can no longer take for granted that our students will read the syllabus outside of class. We must use part of the first or second class meeting to have students work *collaboratively* with the syllabus. Reading the syllabus to them, as I used to do many years ago, will produce glazed looks in your students' eyes. So what I have students do now with my four-page syllabus is work in groups of four, with each student being responsible for one page. I ask each student to teach his or her page to his or her group. After a few minutes of discussion, I reconvene the large class, open the floor up to questions, and—quite often—ask students to explain to their peers the various course requirements and policies.

Joe Cuseo, a psychology professor and director of the freshman seminar program at Marymount College in California, says he distributes the course syllabus on the first day of class but spends no time reviewing it. Instead, he assigns the syllabus as a homework task and deals with it during the second class meeting. He wants students to focus on people rather than paper during the first class session, he stresses. Indeed, Cuseo wants to establish rapport with his students from the very beginning. He uses a "Student Information Sheet" featuring questions the students must answer. Those questions are divided into six general categories:

1. Personal background

2. Future plans

3. Personal abilities, achievements, and distinctive qualities

4. Personal interests

5. Personal values

6. Course expectations and interests

(Note: Cuseo's Student Information Sheet and variations developed by other professors are available on the *On Course Workshop* web site: www.oncourseworkshop.com.)

In addition to being crystal clear about our course expectations, we need to teach students how to do well in our particular courses. In other words, we need to give them study tips. I often assess students' learning styles during one of my early classes in the semester. Students seem to enjoy taking these assessments, which help them discover what kind of learning style they have (visual, auditory, or kinesthetic). Afterwards, we discuss study strategies that will be most effective for the students given their various learning styles. I offer handouts that explain each style and suggest associated study strategies.

I also teach students how to approach the textbook—that is, how to read a chapter quickly at first just to get an overview, then read through it slowly, changing all the titles into questions and looking for the answers. I encourage the students to read with a notebook and pen in hand so they can jot down notes about the material. I often create what I call *objectives booklets* for students, where I outline what information they must know in order to do well. I suggest that they always study with this booklet when they read their textbooks so they can constantly be "looking for the answers." Research tells us that active engagement with material is an effective learning strategy. (I talk more about student engagement and active learning in Chapter 4.)

Given the student diversity in our classes, along so many lines, our task is to offer material in a variety of modes so that we reach as many students as we can. As instructors, we need to educate ourselves on the pedagogical techniques of collaborative learning and the appropriate use of technology to present information. We need to create more interactive mini-lectures, recognizing that the average adult attention span is pretty short. Above all, we need to use variety in our teaching approaches.

We also need to create *learner-centered* classrooms, which I cover in greater detail in Chapter 4. Brown (2005) says that Millennials—or the Net Generation, as he calls them—require a learner-centered model of pedagogy that shifts away from the traditional lecture format and moves toward a more constructivist learning paradigm. This generation of learners, Brown notes, focuses on constructing knowledge using discovery methods and active engagement.

Similarly, Oblinger (2003) points out that today's students have been greatly influenced by information technology. Skiba and Barton (2006) add that Millennials find it helpful when instructors develop a web site for each course they teach. The site might feature class materials, notes, PowerPoint slides, a bibliography of web sources, and other multimedia related to the course. Skiba and Barton emphasize that instructors' web sites must be dynamic—that is, interactive and engaging, not simply static instruments that dispense content. Skiba and Barton also suggest the use of *blogs*, which allow students to interact and engage with the course material and each other. (A blog—short for "web log"—is a web site featuring ongoing, user-generated content that functions as a combination journal and discussion forum. Students can contribute their own content, comment on the content of others, or both.)

Skiba and Barton and other authors suggest the use of simulations, case analyses, and visualizations in class. The bottom line is: You must offer participatory learning for your Millennial/Net Generation students. In Chapter 4, I discuss the changes in pedagogy necessary to engage these students.

Retention and degree completion—
the role of the institution

Let us now explore what institutions of higher learning can do to foster student success and increase degree-completion rates.

First and foremost, institutions must have strong developmental programs for students who need remediation. Many selective four-year institutions have abdicated this role, instead leaving the task in the hands of community colleges. Community colleges are on the forefront of the developmental movement, which is good considering that half of our nation's students start their higher education careers at community colleges. On the other hand, half of our nation's students *do not* start their higher education careers at community colleges—and although they're admitted to four-year institutions, many of them still need to improve their reading, writing, and mathematical skills before they're ready to do college-level work. One sure-fire route to failure is for students to take on college-level work before they have the foundation they need to be successful.

Skiba and Barton (2006) argue that colleges and universities also need to get up to speed in terms of having wired classrooms. Unless technology is readily available to students (and their instructors), the world of academia will seem foreign to today's Millennial students. Of course, *having* the technology is only the first step. Institutions must also provide professional development training so that faculty members know how to *use* new technologies effectively.

Institutions must also capitalize on research findings that demonstrate the benefits of *learning communities*. Learning communities fall along a continuum. At some institutions, a learning community merely means that students are taking linked courses in which instructors from separate disciplines coordinate their classes. At the other end of the spectrum are learning communities in which students take the same classes with a group of their peers. These students often study outside of class together and bond in ways that can be incredibly supportive.

I'm very impressed with the learning communities created by the LISTO program at the College of the Sequoias (COS), forty miles south of Fresno, California (see McGlynn 2006a). LISTO puts students in classes together. Roughly half of COS students are Mexican immigrants or children of Mexican immigrants. Most of them come from families in which the parents are field workers; they have the grueling job of picking fruits and vegetables.

The LISTO program is designed mainly to increase the retention and success of Hispanic and low-income students. Recognizing the need to improve the success of Hispanics—whose college graduation rates lag behind those of every other ethnic group in America—LISTO strives to increase the number of students who transfer to a university at the junior level. Students entering LISTO make a commitment to transfer to a university in two years. The program offers new and returning students a support network of classmates, a retention specialist, and other administrators who monitor students' progress and give them valuable assistance, advisement, mentoring, and encouragement.

Yet another feature that contributes to LISTO's success: it collaborates with students' families. Parents of students are invited to a special parent-student orientation program. While all the attendees hold candles in their hands, a "Promise Ceremony" takes place—during which the students make the following pledge:

> We, the students of the LISTO program, are wholeheartedly committed to our academic success and achievement. We are putting aside some of the complications in our lives to make room for a new beginning—the start of our lives as scholars. We begin our journey with tremendous hope and optimism.

> In the event that we fail to fulfill these promises, we ask your understanding and patience. We are open to receiving your constructive criticism and promise to work diligently to improve on our weaknesses.

Parents, in turn, tell their students (while facing them):

> We promise to assist you in accomplishing the goals you have set for yourself. We will support you when you are down, celebrate your victories when you succeed, encourage you when you have doubts, and rejoice with you as you complete your job as a student.

I understand from LISTO participants that the ceremony is moving, and that it inspires them to try their best.

OTHER INSTITUTIONAL SUCCESS STRATEGIES TO INCREASE MINORITY STUDENT ENROLLMENT, RETENTION, AND DEGREE COMPLETION

A three-year national study of ten predominantly white colleges and universities describes how they experienced dramatic success in graduating minority students over ten or more years (see Richardson and de los Santos 1988). The study was done by the National Center for Postsecondary Governance and Finance and was funded by the U.S. Department of Education's Office of Educational Research and Improvement (OERI). In a nutshell, according to the study, here are the ten success strategies that colleges and universities should implement to improve the graduation rates of minority students:

1. Publicly announce their priorities—that is, they must publicly announce their goal of eliminating racial/ethnic/income disparities in degree attainment and make clear their commitment to educational opportunity.

2. Back up their priorities with a budget that is committed to recruiting, retaining, and graduating minority students.

3. Employ minorities in senior leadership positions—which sends a very clear message about the value of cultural diversity among professional staff.

4. Track institutional progress through effective assessment techniques.

5. Provide comprehensive support services and take a proactive role in offering financial aid to minority students.

6. Emphasize quality and high academic standards.

7. Reach out to community schools, agencies, and businesses to raise minority students' aspirations and academic preparation.

8. Bridge educational gaps by providing extended classes (covering required material), tutoring, strong developmental programs, learning laboratories, collaborative study groups, and intrusive advising.

9. Reward good teaching and diversify their faculties—rewards, tenure, and promotions should hinge on good teaching, characterized by: caring, mentoring, sensitivity to cultural diversity, and high expectations for all students.

10. Create a non-threatening social environment so that minority students feel welcome and included in campus life.

In other words, institutions of higher education need to take a more proactive role if we are to improve the success rate of minority students.

INSTITUTIONAL ACCOMMODATIONS FOR TODAY'S STUDENTS

Diana Oblinger (2003) addresses the implications of differing learning styles and varying degrees of technological literacy among today's students—particularly in terms of the institution's role in meeting students' needs. Many institutions, she notes, are attempting to cater to the customer service mentality of new students by eliminating delays in processes ranging from admissions services to financial aid to academic support. Recognizing that such delays cause dissatisfaction and disengagement among students who are used to 24/7 service, some institutions—such as the University of North Carolina-Greensboro (UNCG)—use online personal assistants, automated e-mail portals, and customized web mail to offer instant responses to students. UNCG also has a "Virtual Information Station," where students can get quick answers to frequently asked questions.

Oblinger further explains that adult learners bring their own customer service expectations to the institutions they attend, and that in many cases these expectations are more a prerequisite than a preference. In fact, Oblinger says, one reason students often give for abandoning their studies is lack of timely support. Oblinger correctly points out that there is no single formula or magic bullet for meeting students' expectations with respect to service, immediacy, and what they perceive to be a stimulating learning environment. There can't be a single formula, she explains, since students represent different generations of learners, differing learning styles, various expectations, and diverse communication preferences.

What Oblinger does recommend is a first step: understanding the "new" learners in terms of generational differences. Who are the older students, the Baby Boomers, the Gen Xers, and the Millennials, and how can we meet the challenges of educating them in our diverse classes? These are the types of challenges this book addresses—starting in depth with Chapter 2, where we compare the generations.

CHAPTER TWO

Comparing Generations of Students

Classifying generations

One common way to classify students according to generation is to look at the years they were born. Oblinger and Oblinger (2005b) have developed a classification system that puts the generations into four categories: Matures (born between 1900 and 1946), Baby Boomers (1946 to 1964), Generation X (1965 to 1982), and the Net Generation/Millennials (1982 to 2002). (Note: The Net Generation/Millennials group is also referred to at times as Generation M, Generation Y, Digital Natives, and the Echo Boomers.) I use these ranges here, although others have made slightly different distinctions.

Richard Sweeney of the New Jersey Institute of Technology (2006) separates the Matures—referred to as Traditionalists in some instances —into two distinct subgroups: the GI Generation (born between 1901 and 1924) and the Silent Generation (1925 to 1945). (Note that Sweeney uses slightly different demarcation dates to describe the generations.) I refer to this population—now ranging in age from their early sixties into their eighties and possibly their nineties—simply as older students.

Each generation covers about a twenty-year span, although—as you can see already—researchers often disagree on start/stop dates. Manning,

Everett, and Roberts (2006) point out that every generation is influenced by a host of factors. Economic conditions, societal norms, political events, major historical crises, and—I will add—styles of parenting all contribute to the shaping of a generation, particularly when it comes to the values of its members.

An important caveat about generalizing

As you read this chapter, please know that I am making generalizations about generations of students. These generalizations probably hold true for the majority of each particular cohort. On the other hand, we must be careful not to pigeonhole people based on age; otherwise, "generation profiles" become just another way of stereotyping people.

As I have certainly witnessed firsthand, many students do not fall into neat generational categories. During some recent semesters, I remember thinking: "This is a so-called Millennial according to her date of birth, yet she seems much more like the students from the 1960s generation." Recognizing the complexity and diversity within the generations—as well as between the generations—ensures we don't overgeneralize.

What the various generations have in common

Each generation usually thinks of its own members as the standard of comparison. (Perhaps we could coin a new term—such as "generational-centrism"—to describe this phenomenon.) Generations also tend to look skeptically at the generations that follow them. Manning et al. (2006) describe this phenomenon as the "these kids today…" attitude. They also note that people who are born on the cusp of two generations may have a blended set of characteristics and share similar traits.

Evidence of using one's own generation as the "standard" is often reflected in people's music preferences. Baby Boomers, for example, love to hear the "oldies" of their generation. The older generation, meanwhile, usually savors the popular standards of the 1940s and 1950s. People of each generation believe that the best music was (is) "their" music. Moreover, people of each generation are often intolerant of the music of the day. The older generation didn't like the Baby Boomers' rock 'n roll. Similarly, many Baby Boomers stopped listening to newer music as it came along.

In my opinion, today's children and college students are exposed to *some* musical lyrics, *some* MTV and YouTube videos, and *some* films that are more sexist, homophobic, racist, and—there are no other words I can think of——more crude and vulgar than anything that showed up in previous generations. Perhaps it's simply my generational (Baby Boomer) bias. On the other hand, it may be evidence that our culture has changed so significantly in the last several decades that younger generations are inundated with ubiquitous negative stimuli.

In my courses, when students would reveal something about themselves during the first class meeting, they would often share their preferences in music. I knew I was being left in the dust when one of my students said he enjoyed music known as "alternative." My instinct was to ask, "Alternative to what?"—but I kept my ignorance to myself. When students asked what type of music I enjoy, I sometimes said I like many types of music (which is true) so that I could avoid acknowledging the cultural divide between us—that is, between the Baby Boomers and the Millennials. In one instance, a student wanted me to be more specific. So I named various genres, such as classical, jazz, popular standards, oldies. I said I like some country, too. I admitted I don't listen to heavy metal or rap.

The student pressed on by asking me if I had a CD player in my car and, if so, what I listened to during my drive to school. I remember the moment vividly because I was so embarrassed by my answer—not because of who the artist is but because I knew the students would see the cultural divide. I sheepishly told the truth: "Dean Martin: Greatest Hits." To my surprise, I realized that the cultural divide was even bigger than I had imagined—for I could tell by my students' expressions that most of them had no idea who Dean Martin was.

Generational comparisons

Some researchers have studied generational differences extensively. Here, I make only cursory comparisons since our classes are diverse in terms of age. But for the most part I concentrate on the Millennials, since they represent the largest proportion of the enrollment swell. I focus on the Millennials for another important reason as well: They seem qualitatively different from the students they are following, and thus our teaching techniques must adapt to how these students learn. Moreover, the Millennials—who first entered college around 1999 and 2000—are second only to the Baby Boomers in terms of their overall numbers.

The challenges of teaching mixed generations in our classes

There are a number of interesting issues related to the impact of generational differences in our classes.

First, since our classrooms are diverse in terms of age—particularly at community colleges—we usually have a mix of generations. This creates significant challenges for us as teachers, not only because of varying levels of maturity and life experience among our students, but also because different generations bring different expectations to the classroom, different attitudes toward the classroom experience, and different learning preferences. Given the age diversity in our classes, it's important that we speak to *all* students as if they are mature adults. From early research (see Rosenthal and Jacobson [1968] and Elliott [1968]), we know that students rise to our expectations both academically and behaviorally. So most Millennials will behave more maturely in class if we make that expectation clear to them.

Second, if we're clear about our course expectations from the very start of the semester—and if we're a bit flexible with regard to students' expectations, such that our own expectations aren't presented as if they're etched in stone—the mix of age levels in class should not present a particular problem. In my own teaching experience as well as that of my colleagues, having people of different ages in class adds spice and richness to the educational environment—especially when students discuss personal life experiences that are relevant to the course material.

Finally, we can address the diverse learning preferences that arise from both innate and experiential (including generational) factors by varying our pedagogical strategies. We need to expand our teaching repertoires so that we bring as many students as possible into the classroom community.

The older generation

Sitting side by side with other generations of students in many of our classes are the Matures or Traditionalists—the ones I refer to simply as older students, ages 61 and up. One of my all-time favorite Mature students was a woman from Russia. Eighty-seven years old, she was an incredibly bright and intellectually curious person.

I mention her attitude toward education to contrast it with those of some of my Millennial students. At the beginning of each semester, I talked about the importance of class attendance. (I taught at a commuter community college. Attendance was often an issue for our students thanks to job conflicts, family obligations, and inclement weather.) One very snowy day, when I had barely made it in to the college myself, I received a voicemail from my older Russian student before class. She told me in her faltering English that she had waited for the bus for an hour and a half, but that the bus had never come. She then apologized for her absence that day. I remember cradling the phone for a minute after listening to that message and thinking to myself, "What an embrace of life, and what a zest for learning!"

The younger members of this older generation—a subgroup referred to as the Silent Generation by Sweeney (2006) and as the Greatest Generation by others—were born between 1925 and 1945. They were the children of the Great Depression and World War II. They developed values of commitment, dedication, conformity, and obedience to rules, law, and authority. Some of them lived through the Stock Market Crash of 1929. After the Great Depression, they lived through the Roosevelt years of the New Deal. They experienced Pearl Harbor, the Holocaust, the end of World War II, the death of Roosevelt, and the Korean War. They had no televisions, but their families listened to the radio together. They also had a strong sense of extended family. In fact, many of them grew up with grandparents living in the home.

The Baby Boomers and the gaps between students and teachers

According to Oblinger and Oblinger (2005b), the Baby Boomers are known as the "Me Generation." I believe this label has been applied because we Baby Boomers have paid quite a bit of attention to "self." Health clubs, spas, and widespread interest in and knowledge of medical matters exemplify Baby Boomers' care for the self. Indeed, Oblinger and Oblinger say many Baby Boomers tend to be optimistic and to become workaholics. They have a sense of responsibility, a strong work ethic, and a "can do" attitude.

What is it that Baby Boomers dislike? "Laziness," according to Oblinger and Oblinger (2005b). I mention this last point because when Baby Boomer teachers deal with Millennial students, the teachers may perceive their Net Gen students as lazy because Net Gen students tend to learn and work differently. For example, I was an incessant note taker as a student. Conversely, some of the students in the classes I taught didn't take notes at all. I would emphasize the importance of note taking not only as an active learning strategy but also as a way of having a record of what class was all about. But some of my students said they learned best by listening and sometimes even taping the classes.

Oblinger and Oblinger (2005b) assert (and I agree) that generational differences may be less influential than people's fluency with technology. In other words, perhaps the differences between Baby Boomers and Millennials have more to do with technological comfort (or discomfort, as the case may be) than anything else. Recently, my Baby Boomer friend asked her Net Gen daughter to help her upload pictures from her camera to her computer. The daughter rolled her eyes and replied, "*M-O-M,* I already showed you how to do that!" Being a Baby Boomer techno-immigrant myself, I loved my friend's response: "Remember how long it took for you to learn which direction the letter J went when you were young?" Even her daughter accepted that "touché."

The reason I mention this technological gap between generations is that it impacts higher education significantly. As Oblinger and Oblinger (2005b) point out, generational issues are significant to higher education because the people running the institution—i.e., the administration, faculty, and staff—may have different technological expertise as well as different life experiences vis-à-vis many of their students.

In many cases, there is also a *cultural* gap between teachers and students that may affect the learning environment. Although Baby Boomers are retiring and making room for younger teachers, we still make up the majority of most college faculties. There was once a time in our lives when we had a sense of "knowing more than our elders"—when we Baby Boomers thought we understood the world and that adults were "out of it." A similar disconnect exists today between many Millennial students and their Baby Boomer parents and teachers. There is, for example, a sense of technological superiority among the "digital natives," who think their parents' and teachers' lack of technological expertise is pathetic, and that their parents' worries about social networking web sites like MySpace and Facebook are unfounded.

Simply put, the Baby Boomer and Millennial generations are from two different worlds in many ways.

The Gen Xers

The Gen Xers, born between 1965 and 1981, came to college for the first time in 1982 and 1983. This cohort followed my own generation, and I had been teaching for about a decade when they arrived on campus.

Gen X is about half the size of the Baby Boomer generation, and it has also been called the Lost Generation and the Nomadic Generation. According to Manning et al. (2006), divorce reached an all-time high in America when Gen Xers were children. The nation witnessed single-parent families becoming the norm for society. Indeed, 40 percent of Gen Xers are children of divorce (Wilson 1998). Their families were often spread out, and they lived in a world that had started to be perceived as unsafe. The term "latch-key kid" was coined to describe the many Gen X children who came home to empty houses after school because their parents—or their single mothers—had to work.

The historical events in the lives of Gen Xers that may have impacted their development include the Watergate scandal, which more than likely contributed to Xers' lack of deep involvement in politics. This generation also saw the beginning of an energy crisis. Remember the lines of cars waiting to get gas on the days they were assigned? Gen Xers witnessed women's liberation protests, the fight for equal gender opportunities, and the eventual fall of the Berlin Wall. Ronald Reagan was inaugurated in 1980. Gen Xers witnessed the emergence of AIDS, and many of them tracked the Iran hostage crisis endlessly on TV. Gen Xers also watched the explosion of the space shuttle Challenger, some experiencing it in real time. John Lennon was shot and killed, an event that crossed several generations in terms of its impact. Gen Xers lived during the Chernobyl nuclear accident, the relatively minor 1987 crash of the U.S. stock market, and the beginning of massive layoffs by American corporations.

Wilson (1998) says that Generation X lacks a defining life event. She calls Gen Xers the MTV generation and notes the names of some of their rock groups: Garbage, Social Distortion, and Fun Lovin' Criminals. She also believes that there is a fundamental pessimism among Gen Xers. Based on her research at two different Midwestern universities, Wilson says that Gen Xers seem to express nostalgia for the past instead of being oriented toward the future. She also points out that Gen Xers came of age during a time when the dual-career family was becoming the norm, the national debt was rising, and the environment was deteriorating—the latter explaining, she believes, why Gen Xers have become environmentally conscious.

Wilson also discusses the work of Conrad Kottak, a professor of cultural anthropology at the University of Michigan and a prolific author. Kottak coined the term "teleconditioning" to refer to television-conditioned behaviors that he says are common among Gen Xers. Kottak believes the TV-watching habit promotes actions that are inappropriate in the college classroom. He cites as examples of these behaviors the tendency for students to enter and leave classrooms at will, to carry on side conversations in class, and to bring food to class. (I'll have more to say about classroom behavior in Chapter 3.)

According to Manning and her colleagues, Gen Xers had to become self-sufficient and pragmatic since they were born at a time when children seemed to be at the bottom of our societal priority list. Thus, they developed into conscientious, bottom-line types who found they could only depend on themselves.

Again, much of this may be true—but beware of generalizations about generations ...

The Millennials/Echo Boomers/Net Generation/ Generation M/Generation Y/Digital Natives

As you can see, the Millennial generation has many other labels as well. Manning et al. (2006) say the Millennials have grown up during the largest financial boom in history. There was steady income growth in America throughout the 1990s, although there was still a great disparity across race/ethnicity lines. Millennials of middleclass and upper-middleclass families became accustomed to getting what they wanted because their parents could afford to lavish them. Despite the economic growth, however, many Millennials saw their parents lose their savings in the dot-com bubble stock market crash of March 2000, as well as the stock market decline following the terrorist events of September 11, 2001.

Millennials are the children of two generations. In the 1980s, Baby Boomers became older parents. Manning (2006) points out that in 1989, almost 30 percent of the 4.4 million live births were to women age thirty or older. Indeed, some women were having their first children in their forties —and with reproductive technologies and adoptions, some Baby Boomers were starting families in their fifties. Millennials, then, are mostly the sons and daughters of Baby Boomers. So their parents tend to be older than those of the teenagers and young adults who came before them:

> The baby boomers generally had children later and in smaller numbers than their prewar generation parents. But when they did start reproducing, from about 1970 to 1995, they did so with a vengeance. The result: the growth in the under-18 population that's already reverberating in classrooms today. (Williamson 2002, 4)

Other demographic trends also describe and/or impact the Millennials. As I noted in Chapter 1, our nation has seen a dramatic increase in Latino/a immigration. Moreover, Latinas have higher birth rates than white women do. The Pew Research Center (Hakimzadeh 2006) notes that by 2005, Hispanics accounted for one out of every five women giving birth in the United States. The result: Today, a little more than one-third of Millennials are non-white or Latino. The Pew report also tells us that, given the large percentage of young Hispanics and their high birth rates, Hispanics will continue to have a major impact on our school systems thanks to the sheer numbers of children they produce.

Moreover, one in five Millennials has at least one parent who is an immigrant. The bottom line: Millennials are the most ethnically and racially diverse generation in our nation's history.

Manning et al. (2006) describe some other interesting demographic trends too. For example, Millennials usually come from smaller families. Only children, once a smaller minority, now comprise about 10 percent of the population in the United States. Although socioeconomic status is often tied to ethnicity/race—and despite the large number of children of immigrants in our schools—Millennials in general have parents who are more educated than the parents of previous generations were. In fact, 25 percent of Millennials have at least one parent who has earned a bachelor's degree or higher. Thanks to the great increase in the number of women in higher education, the Millennials are the first generation whose mothers are more educated than their fathers (albeit by a small margin).

Millennials are also the most protected generation in terms of government safety rules. The Millennials rode in car seats and used safety belts that had to meet government regulations. When I was four or five years old, I had a steering wheel with a rubber sticker on the end of it that attached to the front windshield. I stood up and "steered" the car when my father was driving. The Millennial generation, conversely, is required by law to wear helmets when they ride their bikes. My husband, who is also a Baby Boomer, remembers biking down incredibly steep and trafficked hills; helmets were unheard of. When Millennials go inline skating, they wear kneepads and elbow pads. When I roller skated (earlier in my life!), I had bloody knees all season. Manning and her colleagues (2006) point out that all of these differences probably contribute to the finding that between 1960 and 1997, the mortality rate among American teenagers declined. Millennials are having fewer accidents than we Baby Boomers did. No wonder!

As I discussed in my *Hispanic Outlook in Higher Education* article "Teaching Millennials" (McGlynn 2005):

- Millennials are expected to excel. If they don't—and if their parents have the financial means—they're provided with tutors and coaches. Thus, many of our Millennial college students expect individual attention, extra guidance, and institutional resources that will help them with any difficulties they encounter. (Understanding this phenomenon may ease our frustration with what we sometimes perceive as their sense of entitlement.)

- When Millennial students were growing up, they were highly scheduled; they're used to listening to what their parents say.

- Multitasking is a way of life for the Millennial generation. While some view this activity as a strength, there is a potential downside as well: Many Millennial students believe they can learn complex information while they're listening to music or engaging in other activities.

Wallis et al. (2006) offer an in-depth look at multitasking among the Millennials. The writers note that the Millennials seem to have mastered multitasking in ways that previous generations either admire or disparage. Millennials can be found listening to their iPods, doing their homework, and sending Instant Messages (IM-ing) all at the same time. Although some people see this ability as an asset and believe that Millennials' brains have been altered by experience so that they can pull off multitasking, many cognitive psychologists say the Millennials are sacrificing the quality of their attention by doing two or more things at once. As Wallis et al. put it (52):

> It may seem that a teenage girl is writing an instant message, burning a CD, and telling her mother that she's doing homework—all at the same time—but what's really going on is a rapid toggling among tasks rather than simultaneous processing.

Neuroscientist Jordan Grafman, chief of the cognitive neuroscience section at the National Institute of Neurological Disorders and Stroke, says of multitasking: "You're doing more than one thing, but you're ordering them and deciding which one to do at any one time" (Wallis et al. 2006, 52).

I'm reminded of trying to have phone conversations with my thirteen-year-old goddaughter, knowing she must also be on the computer doing homework or Instant Messaging someone else because I can sense I don't have her complete attention—and she called *me*! This attempt at multitasking is commonplace among Millennials. And as I witness this particular middle schooler multitasking with such proficiency and speed—particularly considering that she's Instant Messaging, a communication form that has its own set of acronyms which eliminate any semblance of full sentence narratives—I predict that the students who enter college four or five years from now will be even more difficult to teach if we continue to rely on traditional teaching methods. Oblinger and Oblinger (2005b) tell us that talking to friends online is the way today's teenagers hang out. Their use of Instant Messaging is a way of life. Indeed, the Oblingers say that today's middle schoolers know more of their friends' screen names than their home phone numbers. When my friend's teenage son had a party at their house, I asked him the name of one of the girls at the party. He told me her screen name and said he didn't know her real name!

Additional Millennial characteristics—ones that may differentiate them from even their own older siblings—are that they gravitate toward group activity; identify with their parents' values and feel close to their parents; believe it's cool to be smart; are fascinated by new technologies; and are racially and ethnically diverse. In her discussion of the work of Claire Raines (2002), Oblinger (2003, 38) notes that:

> ... Millennials exhibit distinct learning styles. For example, their learning preferences tend toward teamwork, experiential activities, structure, and the use of technology. Their strengths include multitasking, goal orientation, positive attitudes, and a collaborative style.

Jason Frand (2000) describes ten characteristics of students who have what he calls an "Information-Age mind-set." Interestingly, he says that today's students don't see computers as technology; they've never known life without computers and the Internet. Rather, Millennials view the computer as an assumed part of life.

Frand also discusses several other Millennial characteristics that have implications on the ways we teach. Among them:

- Doing is more important than knowing. Millennials don't see knowledge as the ultimate goal, especially when the half-life of information is so short.

- Learning more closely resembles Nintendo than logic. Nintendo symbolizes a trial-and-error approach to solving problems. Thus, losing becomes the fastest way to master a game—because losing involves learning. By contrast, previous generations of students took a more logical, rule-based, linear approach to solving problems.

- Staying connected is essential. Students stay in touch using a variety of tools, including cell phones, personal digital assistants (PDAs), and computers. They can connect with each other practically anyplace, anytime.

- There is zero tolerance for delays. Millennial students expect services to be available around the clock and in a variety of modes (e.g., Internet, phone, in person). They also expect response time to be fast.

- The line between consumer and creator is blurring. In a file-sharing, cut-and-paste world, the distinctions between creator, owner, and consumer of information are fading. Often, the operative assumption among Millennials is that if something is digital, it's everyone's property. (Note: This mind-set gives us another perspective on certain aspects of "cheating," a topic I cover in Chapter 3.)

"Helicopter" parents

Manning and her colleagues (2006) say that some parents of today's Millennial college students have been dubbed "helicopter" parents because they "hover" over their children—even their grown, college-age children. These researchers also call some Baby Boomer parents "snowplow parents" because they try to clear the way for their children. In a *USA Today* article entitled "New Baby Boom Swamps Colleges," Anthony DeBarros (2003) writes that Echo Boomers (Millennials) are confident, achievement oriented, and accustomed to having their parents keep very close tabs on them.

Perhaps as a result of being underprotected and underprepared for their own adolescence, many Baby Boomers have become very protective parents themselves. Part of that protectiveness undoubtedly stems from their efforts to keep their children safe in a world that seems increasingly unsafe. Particularly from middle school on—when parents tend to have less control of their children's behavior—many children are surfing the Internet, listening to gangster rap music, watching inappropriately sexual and violent videos, Instant Messaging ad nauseam, and joining social networking sites like MySpace and Facebook that put them in vulnerable situations. Parenting children and adolescents today is a more challenging task in some ways than it was for past generations. It's difficult *not* to hover if you're an active and caring parent.

But some people say that Baby Boomer parents hover over their children a bit *too* much. Baby Boomers made some conscious decisions about how they would parent. Many of them wanted to parent differently than they themselves were parented. Family therapists warn that there is a difference between parenting "differently" and parenting in the *opposite* way. In their attempts to parent differently, some Baby Boomers have leaned too far in the opposite direction of the way they were parented.

Many Baby Boomers were children of parents who were authoritarian. When these Baby Boomers were children, it was their parents' way "or the highway." Authoritarian parents expected blind obedience and said things like, "You will do it because I say so!" Most child development experts see the move away from authoritarianism as healthy. Parenting differently from the authoritarian style would be to parent authoritatively. One very positive distinction between authoritarian parents and authoritative parents is that authoritative parents tend to be much warmer than authoritarian parents are. Authoritative parenting also means that the parents accept and embrace the role of parent; that they realize they are the ultimate decision makers when it comes to their children and teenagers; and that they give their children structure, guidance, and limits. Authoritative parents encourage open communication with their children—unlike their authoritarian predecessors—so that they encourage their children to express their feelings. But authoritative parents also know when to cut off negotiations with their children, and how to set limits in terms of discipline.

In their efforts to be non-authoritarian, many Baby Boomer parents became permissive. They didn't set limits for their children or give them a framework for their behavior. They encouraged full participation in decision making, which has sometimes led to children becoming expert negotiators. (Indeed, some would say that these children are experts at *manipulating* and/or *arguing*.)

On a positive note, Millennials have learned negotiation skills very well, and many of them became decision makers at an early age. Many Baby Boomers, in their noble attempt to form close relationships with their children, abandoned the parenting role in favor of a "buddy" role. For some families, this approach has worked pretty well. For others, it has been less than ideal to say the least.

Obviously, all of these developments have profound implications for today's college classroom, where many Millennials expect to be able to negotiate almost anything—including their grades. And some institutions of higher education are reporting that "helicopter" parents are over-involved with their college students' lives, interfering in the advising and registration process and their students' interactions with professors, classmates, and roommates. Set foot on any college campus today and you'll see students talking on their cell phones; a great number of them are talking with their parents—especially their mothers. Some people have referred to the cell phone as a virtual umbilical cord.

Lest I sound overly critical here, let me acknowledge that there are numerous positive aspects to how many Baby Boomers parent their children. Baby Boomers—particularly fathers—spend more time with their children and teenagers than their own fathers spent with them. Given today's smaller overall family size, each child is getting more attention. Baby Boomer parents and their children appear to have strong social connections, and Millennials seem to share their parents' values. Contrast these characteristics with those of the Baby Boomers as teenagers and young adults. Their motto at the time: "Don't trust anyone over thirty."

One aspect of how many Baby Boomers parent their children that may in fact be a double-edged sword is their emphasis on self-esteem. Many Millennials will tell you that their parents are their biggest fans. These are the parents who learned the importance of self-esteem from a cultural self-esteem *movement*. They learned to say "Good job!" and to dish out praise endlessly. This may have buoyed the Millennials' self-worth and confidence in the short term. But now, some Baby Boomer parents are wondering why their children still have self-esteem issues, particularly during the prepubescent and teenage angst years.

Millennials expect feedback and praise, and it has to be prompt. They'll often misperceive silence or constructive feedback as criticism. Again, the implications for the college classroom are apparent: Millennials want immediate reaction to the work they produce—and they often become demoralized when given less than high praise.

Customer service and sense of entitlement

Many professors complain that their Millennial students seem to have a sense of entitlement—a belief that they have a rightful claim for things to go their way. If there's any truth to this observation—and I believe there is where some of the Millennials are concerned—where does the sense of entitlement phenomenon come from?

Manning and her colleagues (2006) place the Millennial generation into a socio-historical-cultural context. They say that these students expect access to college services and to faculty and staff 24/7 because as consumers that's all they've known. Accustomed to having the ability to call toll-free numbers or visit web sites day and night, they are surprised and frustrated when they don't get immediate answers. My colleagues who teach online courses say that some of their students expect them to be online and available around the clock! Millennials were born into a culture that emphasizes customer service, and many of them have bought into it hook, line, and sinker. In their Introduction for *Educating the Net Generation*, Oblinger and Oblinger (2005a) talk about Millennials' demands for immediate answers. What we Baby Boomers might interpret as impatience is actually, the Oblingers suggest, a part of the Millennials' world of immediacy.

Again, we see differences related to socioeconomic status (SES). Although community colleges have a mix of students in terms of SES, they have greater numbers of first-generation-to-college students and students from lower socioeconomic backgrounds. It is my belief—based on feedback from my colleagues who have taught at both four-year and two-year schools —that the sense of entitlement is more pervasive in the four-year college/ university sector than it is at the community college level. Perhaps the reason is that many community college students have not had things handed to them on a platter—including their education—and that many of them either pay for or contribute toward their own tuition.

The customer service mentality among Millennials also contributes to their increasing propensity to go to more than one college, either consecutively or simultaneously, to earn a degree. Some college officials are calling this "swirling," "mix and match," "cut and paste," "grab and go." In "College, My Way"—an article published in the Education Life section of *The New York Times*—Kate Zernike (2006) reports that this phenomenon fits the Millennial mentality. Today's students, she says, lack brand loyalty, and they're used to having things their own way. Zernike notes that Millennials have a can-do attitude about changing anything they don't like. In Zernike's article, Jacqueline Murphy—director of admissions at St. Michael's College in Vermont—says (24):

> These Millennial kids are the most loved, most wanted kids ever, and they want things to be immediately perfect. ... They want to get things done, and maybe they decide that if things aren't going their way they'd rather be elsewhere where things are going their way. Some of it is: If there's a little adversity or things aren't as promised, I'll take my tent and go elsewhere. ... Personally, I don't think it's the best way to deal with things. In life you have good days and bad days, and learning to establish that even keel is important.

Zernike reports that for many students, moving between different colleges isn't about finding themselves or changing majors; it's about *efficiency*. The 2005 *National Survey of Student Engagement* reveals that about half of college seniors have taken a class elsewhere, and many of them have done so to complete their educational requirements sooner. Remember: Millennials have high expectations for themselves, instilled in them by their parents and the competitive school culture. Part of their "swirling" and "mixing and matching" may stem from lack of satisfaction, as Zernike reports. But these activities may also be a function of Millennials simply trying to get where they're going faster.

Digital natives and digital immigrants

Mark Prensky (2001) coined the comparative phrase "Digital Natives, Digital Immigrants," and it's one I find appealing in comparing generations. Millennials have never known a world without computers; for them —except, perhaps, for some students from lower-socioeconomic-status backgrounds—computer technology is an assumed part of life. Millennials have always used the Internet as their first source of information, even before textbooks. They also use the Internet for interactivity and socializing, preferring the computer over television. Moreover, cell phones are among their most essential tools. Millennials need to stay connected with friends and family. Indeed, it often seems that they're constantly talking on their cell phones (or using them to send text messages).

As I mentioned earlier in this chapter, the Millennials' exposure to technology is so ubiquitous that they don't even perceive the computer as an example of technology.

Think about it: If you came into a world where computers were already an established part of life, your experiences would undoubtedly be very different from those of people who see the personal computer (PC) as a kind of "miraculous" invention.

In "Is It Age or IT: First Steps toward Understanding the Net Generation," Oblinger and Oblinger (2005b) discuss information technology (IT) as it relates to children and teenagers. They tell us that the Millennials started being born around the time the PC was introduced. Twenty percent of the Millennials began using computers between the ages of five and eight. Today's children are starting even younger; it's not uncommon to see toddlers using computers. Earlier generations obtained information through print resources. Millennials are much more likely to go to the computer for it.

As a Baby Boomer, I'm an *immigrant* to the world of technology. I've learned to navigate my way through some technologies—for example, creating PowerPoint presentations, using an iPod and downloading iTunes, and using a digital camera—although in a pretty basic way. Prensky says the rapid dissemination of digital technology has transformed the Millennial generation:

> Today's students—[kindergarten] through college—represent the first generations to grow up with this new technology. They have spent their entire lives surrounded by and using computers, video games, digital music players, video cams, cell phones, and all the other toys and tools of the digital age. ... Computer games, e-mail, the Internet, cell phones, and instant messaging are integral parts of their lives. (Prensky 2001, 1)

Millennials, in other words, are digital *natives*. Manning et al. (2006) tell us that the Millennials have been "plugged in" since they were babies. They've grown up in a world of computer games and educational software.

Prensky says that, given the digital environment of Millennial learners and how much they interact with that environment, "Today's students process information fundamentally differently from their predecessors" (Prensky 2001, 1). His camp believes that experience has physically reshaped the brains of the Millennial generation. There is some support for this notion. Prensky notes that even if we can't be certain that Millennials' brains have been physically altered through life experience, we do know that their thinking patterns have changed. Digital natives are used to receiving information extremely quickly. They enjoy multitasking and parallel cognitive processing—that is, thinking of more than one thing at a time. The Millennials, Prensky says, prefer what he calls "random access"—like hypertext. Hypertext allows the Millennials (all of us, actually) to go from web site to web site with just the click of a mouse. Prensky says the Millennials also prefer to view graphics before reading text. Moreover, they seem to function best when networked; they thrive on frequent rewards and instant gratification; and they prefer playing games to doing serious work.

The analogy that Prensky uses for digital immigrants is a compelling one. He says that those of us who weren't born into the digital world but who have adapted to it somewhat will still always be immigrants. We will always have the immigrant's "accent," no matter how technologically savvy we think we've become. The digital natives will always recognize us as foreigners in *their* world.

What is the rub for effective education, according to Prensky? In his words (2001, 2):

> … [T]he single biggest problem facing education today is that our Digital Immigrant instructors, who speak an outdated language (that of the pre-digital age), are struggling to teach a population that speaks an entirely different language.

The digital natives are well aware of this disconnect. When they arrive at college, Millennials often feel as if they've entered a culture of heavily accented, unintelligible foreigners who lecture them. How many times have we immigrants used phrases in class like "I must sound like a broken record"? Colleagues have shared with me their own children's disappointment with college. These young people have been accepted to elite, selective institutions, only to complain to their parents that their professors come into the room to "talk at them," leave, and then assign a graduate assistant to stay afterward to address students' questions. How do these emerging adults sum up the college experience? Many of them say their classes are boring, not creative, and not fun.

The problem, Prensky points out, is that we digital immigrants are often reluctant to change our ways. We don't always appreciate the skills acquired by the natives, and we sometimes disparage what the natives have learned through years of digital interaction and practice. We want the new

59

students to learn the way we did—step by step, in a logical order, individually. That's just not the way of our new world. As Prensky puts it (2001, 3):

> Unfortunately for our Digital Immigrant teachers, the people sitting in their classes grew up on the "twitch speed" of video games and MTV. They are used to the instantaneity of hypertext, downloaded music, phones in their pockets, a library on their laptops, beamed messages and instant messaging. They've been networked most or all of their lives. They have little patience for lectures, step-by-step logic, and "tell-test" instruction.

So who has to change? Often, we Baby Boomer professors believe we own the academic culture, and that it's our job to help new students assimilate. There is some truth to this attitude in that we professors need to guide students toward becoming critical thinkers and developing information literacy. We need to teach our students the difference between reliable sources of information and less credible ones. And of course we need to share with our students the content of our disciplines. But as Oblinger and Hawkins (2005, 13) ask:

> What is the proper balance between student and faculty perspectives? Although listening to learners is important, faculty and administrators are experts in their disciplines, as well as in how the discipline should be taught. On what subjects should the input of students be sought? In which areas should faculty have the dominant voice?

According to Prensky's native/immigrant analogy, teachers—the immigrants—must do the changing in terms of *how* they reach their students. He rhetorically asks whether natives ever change to accommodate the immigrant population. According to Prensky, immigrants must assimilate into the new culture.

But although Timothy VanSlyke (2003) says Prensky's native/immigrant concept can help us understand the differences between those who are comfortable with technology and those who are not, he takes issue with some of Prensky's conclusions about the way we view teaching and learning. First, VanSlyke rightly questions whether all students are in fact digital natives. As I mentioned previously, socioeconomic status and age play big roles in how much exposure students have had to information technology.

Prensky is a proponent of educating the new generation of students through gaming. VanSlyke agrees with Prensky that we can learn from understanding the native/immigrant divergence of cultures; that education needs to adapt and evolve with changing times; and that educators need to understand the learning styles of their students. He takes issue, however, with one of Prensky's major assumptions: VanSlyke doesn't believe that the new digital native students are incapable of learning from or communicating with digital immigrants. Not all students, VanSlyke argues, fit Prensky's depiction of today's student as being glued to a computer or TV screen. VanSlyke says the typical classroom is much more diverse, with students from different backgrounds and generations. He also stresses that many of today's students lack computers at home (this is true for lower-socioeconomic-status students in particular), that some students have disabilities, and that some simply dislike computer games.

Another significant departure VanSlyke makes with Prensky is that he doesn't believe digital immigrants must learn to speak a new language to be effective teachers. Many teachers, he says, have adopted new, engaging instructional methods that are student centered and that promote active learning—with or without the use of computers. He believes the incorporation of technology into the learning process must be context specific and driven by the particular circumstances of a given course.

Digital natives:
Techno-savvy, yet intellectually naïve?

Oblinger and Hawkins (2005) discuss some additional characteristics of the Net Generation that we need to consider.

Although we know our students may not need to consult an instruction manual to operate an electronic gadget—that such an undertaking is somehow intuitive to them—their comfort level with technology may not be synonymous with technological *competency.* I'm reminded that when I got my iPod, I couldn't figure out how to change the volume. I was looking for buttons or scroll icons similar to those on my cell phone. At the time, my goddaughter was twelve years old. I asked her to show me how to adjust the volume. It never would have occurred to me to slide the wheel of the iPod face. Somehow, these kinds of tasks are either obvious to the younger generation or—since the Millennials are so socially connected—someone immediately showed them how to do the tasks. They just know how to work these contraptions. But as Oblinger and Hawkins (2005) point out, their understanding of technology may be quite shallow.

Additionally, Millennials may not be adept at distinguishing between reliable and unreliable sources of information. Our students may be wizards at computer games, yet not know the difference between a Google search and a search of scholarly, peer-reviewed, juried journals. In Chapter 3, we'll discuss the younger generation's naiveté when it comes to issues of intellectual property; many in this younger generation seem to have difficulty evaluating the credibility and validity of the sources they use. As Oblinger and Hawkins (2005, 12) put it: "The Net Generation may be simultaneously ahead of and behind earlier generations." In Chapter 1, we discussed the demographics of today's college students. Given the prevalence of nontraditional students in our classes, Oblinger and Hawkins (2005, 12) warn us: "To assume that all students are technologically savvy members of the Net Generation would be incorrect."

Regarding the issue of who needs to change given our new students' backgrounds, experiences, and expectations, Manning and her colleagues (2006) say that, at the very least, faculty need to enter the Millennials' world by communicating with them via e-mail, using well-constructed PowerPoint presentations at least some of the time, and giving their students access to online resources and Internet activities. (Note: I emphasize "well-constructed PowerPoint presentations" because in "IT Myths: The Myths about Students," Oblinger and Hawkins [2005] wonder whether "death by PowerPoint" has replaced "death by lecture.") Manning et al. say that many Millennials expect electronic discussion boards and what have been called "smart classrooms"—wired facilities where teachers literally have the Internet and a computer at their fingertips on the front screen.

I believe that Manning et al. represent a reasonable middle ground with respect to digital immigrants needing to change. Yes, we must grow with the times and learn new skill sets (to use today's jargon). But it is still possible to be an effective teacher with today's students using a *variety* of pedagogical strategies that are not necessarily digital. In fact, in *Educating the Net Generation*, Moore, Moore, and Fowler make an important observation (2005, 1):

> Surveys of Net Generation students suggest that their learning experiences reflect mixed technology usage at best, and at worst they may experience ineffective or inappropriate uses of technology in their academic programs.

Moore et al. also discuss the importance of faculty development in teaching Millennial students. As faculty members, we must learn how to effectively use technologies in our teaching practices and improve our understanding of how today's students learn.

Oblinger (2003) suggests several teaching practices that can engage the Net Generation. She discusses simulations to help students visualize complex systems, and she suggests taking advantage of games that involve problem solving and decision making. Games can tap into Millennials' desire for speed and a sense of urgency, which in turn can foster their motivation. And, of course, the use of web sites, chat rooms, blogs, and other appropriate Internet tools can all contribute to our younger students' desire to employ technology and stay connected with other students and their teachers. Moreover, many Millennials lean toward hands-on experiential learning activities.

Manning and her colleagues (2006) emphasize that Millennials want to understand *why* they're doing what they're doing. They want rationales, and they want to have input into their classes. They don't like mundane work, either; they want to be involved in meaningful activities. Thus, they tend to respond well to learning communities and service learning.

Millennials appreciate clear expectations and explicit syllabi. They want to know exactly what will be covered on tests and how they can earn an A. Many professors are annoyed by the question, "Is this on the test?" But if we see this type of concern as part of this generation's need to achieve and do well—and not simply as disinterest in the course material—we will likely not be as frustrated. Because of their high (and sometimes unrealistic) expectations for themselves, not to mention the phenomenon of grade inflation, we also see that some Millennial students become demoralized if they earn a B or a C. During one recent semester, I received an irate e-mail from a student who had earned a B+. He provided a lengthy argument on why he deserved an A. I was a bit surprised given that I thought the B+ was quite generous.

First-generation students and lower-socioeconomic-status students

Like so many other differences between students whose parents are college educated and middleclass and first-generation-to-college students who may be from lower-socio-economic-status households, educational opportunities are not fairly distributed across the groups. As I mentioned earlier, first-generation students and lower-income students are probably not digital natives. If they're from poorer schools, their experience with technology may be extremely limited. Manning and her colleagues (2006) say that there is a huge digital divide between the haves and the have-nots based on income levels and social class.

Thus, what we've discussed here about Millennials may not be true for all students born between 1982 and 2002. First-generation students and students from lower socioeconomic backgrounds probably feel more like immigrants in a foreign land than we can imagine.

The next chapter addresses the kinds of behaviors that can get in the way of the teaching and learning process where today's students are concerned. How can we prevent these behaviors from occurring in the first place, and how can we respond to them if they do occur? Chapter 3 offers strategies that will help you effectively address these critical questions.

CHAPTER THREE

Preventing and Dealing with Disruptive Classroom Behavior

"Are Social Norms Steadily Unraveling?" Apparently they are, according to a recent analysis of six decades' worth of research (Jayson 2006). The analysis suggests that young people today are less concerned about social approval and society's standards than were their peers of past generations. In *Millennials Rising*, Neil Howe and William Strauss (2000) predicted that children born after 1982 would grow up to become America's next "Greatest Generation." The Millennials have also been referred to as the smartest generation of Americans. But recent research challenges these labels and suggests that the Millennials are too self-focused to achieve greatness. Future historians will tell us which perspective is closer to the truth.

In her book *Generation Me*, Jean Twenge (2006), associate professor of psychology at San Diego State University, compares generations born in the 1970s, 1980s, and 1990s. (In 2006, that means people between the ages of about seven and thirty-six.) Twenge's findings suggest that young people (those we call Gen Xers and Millennials in this book) don't care as much about making good impressions or displaying courtesy as their parents and grandparents did when they were growing up.

Twenge's research is unique in that she summarizes large amounts of data collected at different times. Tapping into various tools—including the Marlowe-Crowne Social Desirability Scale, a social science measurement standard—Twenge was able to gather data about Baby Boomers, for example, when they were young in the 1960s and 1970s rather than retrospectively. She then compares what the Baby Boomers were like then with the way young people from other generations are/were. And since the data she analyzes come from anonymous pencil-and-paper answers rather than interview data, her research minimizes the possibility that people simply respond to questions differently these days as compared to yesteryear.

Twenge believes that the cohort she has dubbed "Generation Me" takes it for granted that the self comes first; today's young people, she suggests, are more disrespectful of authority and more depressed than the young people of previous generations. Why are they depressed? According to Twenge's scholarly, data-based research, Gen Xers and Millennials have been raised to aim for the stars by their esteem-building parents and the culture—at the very time when the world is becoming more competitive. Depression emerges from this dissonance.

Incivility vs. obliviousness

From this perspective, the "incivility" we face in today's college classroom may be a function of the new, more relaxed norms regarding courtesy combined with students' recognition of the gap between their expectations and the reality of the academic world.

In my years in the classroom, I noticed that what we often label as "disrespectful" or "rude" behavior among our younger students is actually *obliviousness* to the norms about courtesy—not a deliberate *rejection* of them. For example, students who come into class late and walk in front of the professor to get a seat can easily be seen as impolite. In my experience, however, most of these students don't even know it's rude to walk directly in front of the instructor while he or she is teaching.

In my book *Successful Beginnings for College Teaching* (2001), I offered a chapter entitled "Dealing with Incivility in the College Classroom." In that chapter, I referred to Richardson's (2000) view that the very term "incivility" is ambiguous. Richardson argues that the difficulty of defining incivility is rooted in people's differing personal expectations about what appropriate classroom behavior is. I agree that much of the difficulty we see in today's college classrooms—where and when it occurs—is a product of conflicting expectations between faculty members and students.

The teacher-student expectations gap and sources of anger

In their STARLINK satellite broadcast entitled *Cooperation, Compassion, and Civility in the Classroom*, psychologists Carol Tavris and Elliot Aronson (2003) discussed the divide we often see between student and teacher expectations. In their presentation, Tavris and Aronson examined the cognitive sources of anger—what are we *thinking* that causes us to become angry?

Tavris and Aronson described three sources of anger. The first relates to perception. When I get angry after I spot a sleeping student, for example, how am I interpreting that student's behavior? In my own experience, many years ago, I would sometimes think, "This student is bored to tears, not interested in this course, and I am doing a lousy job." This would lower my self-esteem and I would get upset. When I checked my perception by speaking to the student after class, however, I was amazed at how far off the mark I could be. More often than not, sleeping students would tell me they were doing shift work and that they had come to class right after work—or that they were on medication for some very legitimate reason.

How we perceive "reality" influences how we *experience* our lives. If we can remember that our feelings are often based on how we're framing things cognitively, we'll be able to become more aware of how our perceptions lead to our feelings and our responses to those feelings.

The second source of anger, according to Tavris and Aronson: unmet expectations. Having our expectations thwarted can make any of us angry. Students, for instance, can become angry when their expectations about college and their abilities to do the work are out of sync. Teachers, meanwhile, can become angry when their expectations about students' academic performance or behavior go unmet.

Finally, the third source of anger, say Tavris and Aronson, is a sense of injustice. In other words, we get stuck in our own ideas about how other people *ought* to behave.

Many students experience the college classroom as a foreign place, note Tavris and Aronson—a place where they have to take exams and they don't know the subject or the rules. The culture of the classroom, the researchers say, can generate anger and incivility, often caused by differences in teachers' and students' expectations on key issues. One such disconnect is the gap between how teachers and students feel regarding the purpose of education: Teachers typically think in terms of students becoming educated, while today's students often feel that the purpose of college is to position oneself for a good job after graduation.

Moreover, according to Tavris and Aronson, teachers and students tend to have different ideas about the norms of correct classroom behavior. Students have always brought their prior experiences with teachers and school to the college classroom. Today, note Tavris and Aronson, there has been a "sea change" in our culture such that it's now considered appropriate to express one's anger. Similarly, according to Tavris and Aronson, how students experience the classroom is a function of how connected they feel to the institution, one another, their teachers, and the material they're learning.

In my thirty-five years of teaching, I found most students to be respectful and well behaved. I also observed, however, that behavior patterns started to change with the Gen Xers and seemed to change even more when the Millennials came onto the academic scene. My colleagues and I often discussed the differences in student behavior, and sometimes we would label that behavior as "inappropriate" and/or "rude." What I've now come to understand, though, is that the behaviors we as teachers perceive as rude are frequently not *meant* to be rude. Often, we're simply looking at the effects of a cultural divide—particularly between Baby Boomer teachers and today's Millennial students.

That said, I do believe there needs to be a meeting of the minds between faculty and their students, and I think both teachers and students must change. I'll discuss the kinds of changes in the pages that follow, and I'll also address how to handle specific types of student behavior. At this point, let me say that teachers have the task of helping their students assimilate, behavior-wise, into the world of academia. Our expectations as instructors must be clear from the start of the semester. But the *way* we set the tone for the term will impact students' behavior. Hardliner teachers who have an authoritarian style toward students will be the ones most likely to elicit incivility in the classroom.

I've also found that the majority of students who are well behaved in class are themselves bothered by the behaviors of students who are disruptive. Students seem to be just as annoyed as teachers—perhaps more so in some cases—when a cell phone goes off in class, when students come in late, or when students walk in and out of the class for no apparent reason. The class is interrupted—*disrupted*—by these types of behaviors, and the well-behaved students are concerned as much as we are.

Historical background on student behavior

In 2000, the Millennial Generation was just entering college. But concerns about undesirable classroom behaviors predate the arrival of the Millennials. In *Successful Beginnings for College Teaching* (McGlynn 2001), I discussed the work of Schneider (1998), who described Kathy Franklin's research on the history of undergraduate life. Franklin, an assistant professor of higher education at the University of Arkansas at Little Rock, says students have been misbehaving on college campuses for centuries. She discusses thirteenth-century students at the University of Bologna who beat their professors if they didn't like their grades. She also describes Yale University in the 1820s, where students rebelled against classes they found too demanding by throwing plates and food at professors in the dining hall.

What's happening on today's campuses is not unusual, Franklin concludes. But she does argue that students today (keeping in mind that "today" means pre-1998, since Schneider wrote her piece in 1998) are different from the students of ten or more years ago because of demographic changes, consumerism, and their K-12 experiences. Today we're into the second half of the first decade of the new millennium. Franklin's words still ring true—only they resonate even more given this new generation of students. We can even add a few influences to those described by Franklin: namely, the way today's students have been parented, the effects of technology, and the many changes in the fabric of our culture that Millennials have experienced.

Influences on student behavior

SENSE OF ENTITLEMENT

What Peter Sacks (1996) said about Generation X—that their incivility was caused by their consumer attitude—may be even truer for the Millennials. Millennials see themselves as "customers" and have a mind-set of "the customer is always right." Many Millennials bring this mind-set to their higher education pursuits. They believe that since they're paying tuition—or, more likely, their parents are—they should run the show. In short, they often feel that as customers they have the right to behave as they wish—the *entitlement* mentality.

Not all students misbehave out of a sense of entitlement, however. Many of my colleagues believe that the most disruptive behavior occurs in developmental courses. Faculty who teach these courses often have the challenge of socializing their students— many of them first-generation students from lower-income families—to adapt to college norms. By the time they're into college-level courses, many of these students have learned the behavioral guidelines of the academic culture.

As I mentioned in Chapter 2, a sense of entitlement may affect certain sectors of higher education more than others. One possible explanation: the socioeconomic status of students' families. For example, I saw less of the entitlement attitude among my community college students than many of my colleagues see at four-year schools. In fact, when I interviewed several colleagues who had started teaching at four-year institutions and then transferred to community colleges (McGlynn 2004b), some discussed the issue of entitlement. One colleague put it this way:

> Students at four-year colleges whose parents are paying high tuitions for their education often have a sense of entitlement when it comes to grades. When students pay their own way or significantly contribute to their tuition payments, as many community college students do, they are less likely to take their education for granted. At four-year colleges, there are some students who act as if classes are what they do inbetween fraternity parties. In fact, I once had a student who said to me that I needed to give him an A so that he could stay in his fraternity. (McGlynn 2004b, 20)

As more middleclass and upper-middleclass students begin the higher education journey at the community college level, these institutions will probably see more of the entitlement attitude among their student bodies. My hunch, though, is that the issue will always be a bigger one at four-year institutions—particularly expensive, private schools. Although community colleges serve a diverse student body that cuts across all socioeconomic sectors, racial/ethnic groups, and levels of preparedness to do college-level work, I believe the community college sector will continue to provide second chances for people who need them. These students usually have more gratitude for the opportunities that higher education affords them. Indeed, rather than a sense of entitlement, many community college students exhibit what one of my colleagues calls the "triumph of the human spirit over adversity."

Those of us teaching in community colleges have heard stories of triumph from our students that not only inspire us but also make us feel exceedingly privileged. I've heard such stories from my own students, my colleagues, and students I've met in my travels to other community colleges. In my own classes, I've taught students who have overcome drug addiction and turned their lives around; students who have been diagnosed with various types of cancer and have fought it heroically; students who have gotten past severe emotional problems; students who are homeless; and students who are victims of abuse. I've had students who are taking care of terminally ill parents and, of course, many students who are juggling all kinds of intense family and job responsibilities. And they still showed up for class, did the work, and enthusiastically pursued their academic dreams! For so many community college students, the sense of entitlement is a foreign concept.

The Diversity of the Classroom

I believe that diversity in the college classroom enhances the learning experience for everyone, enriching the classroom dialogue and teaching students to appreciate other people and other perspectives. I also believe, however, that diversity may be a contributing factor to the disruptive behavior exhibited by some students.

The diversity in our classrooms with respect to ethnicity/race, gender, age, and social class, while greatly contributing to and enhancing the quality of higher education, may also mean that different groups of students have different expectations about the classroom experience. For example, our older-generation students—those who are back in school after a long time out—may have certain expectations about how the class ought to be run and how students should behave. They may expect you to lecture and for students to sit quietly and take notes. Older returning students may bring to the classroom a seriousness about education and a determination to learn. Many native-born Asian students may have similar expectations. Within many Asian cultures, in fact, respectful classroom behavior is silence. Asking and responding to questions is outside their cultural norm.

On the other hand, Millennials who are fresh out of high school may bring a kind of high school mentality to college. Often their behavior is a sign of immaturity. These students sit side by side with students of other generations. The challenge for us as teachers is to create an atmosphere where *all* of these students feel respected and validated.

The Classroom Format

On many college campuses today, particularly at research universities, classes are taught in a large-lecture format. There may be anywhere from one hundred to fifteen hundred students in a classroom. At one elite university (which I will not name), students take a class in a huge lecture hall where the professor is on stage; many of the students, unable to actually see the teacher, watch him or her on TV monitors.

There are many pitfalls to the lecture format. I'll discuss the academic pitfalls later, in Chapter 4. For now, I'd like to focus on how the large-lecture format encourages disruptive behavior.

In *Successful Beginnings for College Teaching* (2001), I discussed the work of social psychologists Philip Zimbardo (1970) and Steven Prentice-Dunn and Ronald W. Rogers (1989). When people lose a sense of self—that is, when they feel anonymous in a large crowd—the resulting sense of *deindividuation* (a term used by social psychologists to describe the phenomenon) can promote aggressive and undesirable behavior (Diener, Lusk, DeFour, and Flax 1980). Students can easily feel this anonymity, and rightfully so. As a graduate student, I once took an elevator with one of my large-lecture professors. It was the eeriest feeling knowing that the professor had no clue I was in her class.

It's not only the sense of anonymity that can fuel disruptive behavior in large-lecture classes. It's also the fact that the average adult attention span is about twenty minutes. Most lectures are fifty to seventy-five minutes long. Unless the instructor has mastered the art of the interactive lecture—which I describe in Chapter 4—the combination of deindividuation and lack of concentration makes it easy for students to engage in side conversations, text message each other, pass notes, surf the Internet on their laptops, or walk in and out of the lecture hall.

The most important aspect of the incivility issue—
Preventing it in the first place

SETTING THE TONE

There are two multifaceted rules of thumb when it comes to preventing classroom incivility in the first place. The first is to tap your "expert" power by knowing your content, being very well prepared for class, defining and modeling appropriate behavior for your students, and being available and approachable. The second is to use the classroom dynamics to empower students and ensure they all feel valued and welcome in your class. If students feel valued and respected by their teachers and by their fellow students, they'll be much less likely to misbehave. As teachers, we set this tone of respect in the way we listen to and treat our students.

For an in-depth discussion of setting an appropriate tone and classroom dynamic, see "Creating a Welcoming Classroom Environment," Chapter 3 of my book *Successful Beginnings for College Teaching* (McGlynn 2001). Suffice it to say here that teachers who demonstrate respect and caring for their students are much less likely to be confronted by disrespectful, uncaring students than are teachers who create an authoritarian classroom dynamic and who are sarcastic and belittling with their students. In Chapter 3 of *Successful Beginnings*, I suggest strategies for connecting with students and building rapport with them. Among those strategies: learning students' names, using their names in class in ways that boost their self-esteem, and greeting students either individually or as a class before every session. Simply showing genuine interest in your students' learning—and in their lives—can go a long way toward preventing disruptive classroom behavior.

WHY PREVENTION MAY NOT WORK

Students and teachers bring to the classroom certain issues—baggage from their earlier educational and home experiences, perhaps, or certain attitudes, or certain personality traits—that may lead to incivility. Indeed, some classroom behavior difficulties are unpreventable. That said, is it possible that some of us as faculty sow the seeds for disruptive behavior and exacerbate it when it does occur?

Yes. There's no doubt about it. The panelists in the videoconference *Faculty on the Front Lines: Reclaiming Civility in the Classroom* (Amada et al. 1999) did not say that faculty members actually create classroom incivility. They did suggest, though, that the behavior of some college teachers may set the stage for disruptive behavior among students. To cite an example: Teachers who are repeatedly late for class themselves set a bad example for tardy behavior. Students lose respect for such teachers and often start walking in even later than the instructor does.

Other teacher behaviors that may promote student incivility are arrogance, condescension, and sarcasm. Showing students disrespect in any of these ways will probably promote hostility among them. It is imperative that we as teachers create a classroom atmosphere that is welcoming, safe, and inclusive.

Boice (1996) suggests that how we as teachers present ourselves on the first day of class may influence the level of classroom civility. Boice conducted a five-year study of classroom incivility at a large, public university in an urban setting. He found that classroom incivility was quite common, occurring in more than two-thirds of the courses he tracked! Incivility, he discovered, was greatest in classes where students perceived the teacher as aloof and indifferent to student needs. He concluded that the key initiator of classroom incivility was the teacher's lack of expressions of warmth and approachability—what Boice called lack of "immediacy." In my own research, students overwhelmingly report that the approachability of the teacher is a key factor that influences their attitude toward the course.

Both students and faculty present themselves to each other when the semester begins. As I discussed earlier, students and teachers bring baggage to the classroom, not to mention their personalities, their issues, and their conflicts. As if all that weren't enough, we all bring our cultural perceptions and expectations to the classroom as well. While this book focuses mostly on generational perceptions and expectations, we cannot ignore the other highly influential factors related to culture—gender, race/ethnicity, social class, and sexual orientation—that combine with age to create divides or, in some cases, affinities.

THE ROLE OF CULTURAL EXPECTATIONS

In her essay "Understanding Classroom Incivility," Mia Alexander-Snow (2005) discusses cultural perceptions and expectations and poses the question, "Is there greater likelihood for female faculty and faculty of color to experience classroom incivility than their white male counterparts?"(Alexander-Snow 2005, 27).

Alexander-Snow, who also wrote "Dynamics of Gender, Ethnicity, and Race in Understanding Classroom Incivility" (2004), builds on Boice's (1996) premise about how a teacher's lack of warmth and approachability can cause incivility—by adding a cultural context dimension to the classroom. In other words, even in a class where the instructor demonstrates warmth and approachability, students may very well bring to the setting their own preconceived notions about teachers. Alexander-Snow says that the teacher-student sense of "immediacy"—what Boice calls warmth and approachability—may thus be greatly influenced by cultural expectations that are defined by cultural norms, expectations, and stereotypes.

Alexander-Snow (2005) discusses the factors that may affect the classroom dynamic. She questions not only how cultural perceptions impact teacher-student interactions but also who wields the power in class and how that power base affects classroom behavior. Alexander-Snow's analysis is based on concepts drawn from the fields of cross-cultural communication and social theories. She suggests that female instructors and teachers of color may face particularly challenging classroom dynamics. She looks at examples illustrating the indirect influence that cultural perceptions, defined by stereotypes and social power, may have in promoting classroom incivility. I touched on this same phenomenon in *Successful Beginnings* (2001, 102) when I said:

> There are many well-documented cases of students who have challenged and harassed their professors. In some cases, the gender or race/ethnicity of the faculty member may have been a factor that contributed to the student's rudeness. In *The Chronicle of Higher Education*, Schneider (1998) reported the case of a black, female professor who tried to speak to students after class because they had engaged in very disruptive behavior during the class session. The students had been reading newspapers, talking loudly, and passing around a game of tic-tac-toe while she was trying to con-

duct class. When she spoke to the young men after class about their behavior, one of them responded with an extremely vulgar gesture. The teacher interpreted the act as a defiant one, with sexist and racist components.

Since the publication of *Successful Beginnings*, colleagues have offered me firsthand examples of incivilities that seemed to be a product of racism and/or sexism. One female math professor who taught calculus, both introductory and higher-level courses, told me she constantly had to prove herself to her mostly male students—every semester. Her students tended to hold on to the old stereotype that math is a male domain. Another colleague, who is Jewish, told me she overheard an anti-Semitic remark one of her students made to his classmates about her. An Indian professor who teaches English courses and speaks impeccable English told me that students challenged her credentials to teach English nearly every time she walked into a new course. Many women of color have shared similar stories about being treated with a lack of respect by their students.

We need to recognize, however, that this is not all about how students perceive their teachers. Alexander-Snow outlines how we all have multiple cultural identities—including our age, race/ethnicity, social class, and sexual orientation—that differentiate us from others. These cultural identities affect how we see and define ourselves as well as how we interact with others. So we as teachers also bring to the classroom our own sets of identities and perceptions of others based on our own group memberships.

All of this tells us that the factors contributing to classroom dynamics are multiple, complicated, and interactive. The more we know about these factors, the better we'll be able to change the classroom dynamic and move it toward an environment of respect. Understanding that students bring to the classroom preconceived notions that have nothing to do with us personally will be difficult given that students perceive us based on our ascribed characteristics, such as gender, race/ethnicity, and perhaps age as well. But that is our task if we want to maintain our dignity and professionalism.

In the STARLINK video broadcast entitled *Coping with Classroom Incivilities: Nanny 9-1-1 for the Professor*, Stacie Chismark, Laura Duvall, and Mia Alexander-Snow (2005) offered some strategies for mitigating classroom incivility that relate to issues of culture and power. They suggested that we as teachers constantly assess the classroom climate; that we expect to meet some degree of incivility from time to time; and that we recognize how cultural perceptions defined by stereotypes will influence classroom dynamics and the levels of intimacy that are achievable between the teacher and students and among the students themselves.

In cases where students are disrespectful toward us or their classmates, we're often caught totally off guard. However, Amada, Jurhee, Middendorf, Poindexter, and Koffler (1999) suggest in general that we not ignore disrespectful or disruptive behavior. Ignoring disruptive behavior may give the wrong message not only to the offending student but also to the witnessing students. The implicit message you send if you ignore disruptive behavior is that you tolerate it—maybe even *condone* it. So when disruptive behavior occurs, we must address it.

How we address it is another important factor in discouraging future disruptive behavior. We must always show students respect even if we abhor their behavior. We are modeling civility. Avoiding direct confrontation with a student, particularly during the class meeting, is usually the best approach. We need to find ways to address the behavior and have it stop without the student feeling diminished. I have found that sometimes, it works quite well to have a conversation with a disruptive student privately—after class—so I can attempt to elicit their empathy for me and for their classmates. For one of the most common distractions in the classroom—side conversations—I often say that I understand how difficult it is to refrain from side conversations during class. I then share with the students that it's difficult for me to concentrate when other people are talking, and that as such their classmates are likely being distracted as well.

The flip side of what I've proposed here is just as true. While we as faculty members (and institutions) can sometimes set the stage for incivilities, we can also take proactive steps to reduce them or even prevent them in the first place.

The role of clear expectations— academic and behavioral

In *Successful Beginnings for College Teaching* (McGlynn 2001), I discussed two authors whose ideas still hold up today. The work of Amada (1999) and Richardson (2000) weaves together some important suggestions for setting clear expectations and thus reducing the chances of incivility. First and foremost, we need to put into writing what the course expectations are and what *our* expectations are with respect to student behavior. Whether this information is part of the syllabus, an addendum to the syllabus, or a separate guidelines sheet, you should distribute and then discuss it during the first or second class meeting of the semester.

In his book *Coping with Misconduct in the College Classroom: A Practical Model*, Amada (1999) discusses the importance of setting clear academic standards as a basis for evaluating students, and of specifying behavioral standards for class sessions. Most institutions have a code of student behavior that is clearly stated in the student handbook. Be sure you know your school's code so that you'll be better prepared to deal with violations of it if they occur in your classroom.

Richardson (2000) reinforces the idea of spelling out your expectations for acceptable student behavior. In fact, he believes the key contributor to student incivility in the classroom is lack of congruence between student and teacher expectations. He cites five ways that incivility might develop in your classroom:

- You fail to communicate your expectations to the students.
- Your students ignore or disagree with the expectations you've set.
- Your students fail to communicate *their* expectations to you.
- You ignore or disagree with the expectations your students have set.
- Your students disagree with or are unaware of each other's expectations.

Therefore, one way to encourage your students to behave appropriately in the classroom is to be on the same page as they are where expectations are concerned. In *Successful Beginnings for College Teaching*, I offered a "Guidelines for Courtesy and Respect" sheet that was adopted by a committee I chaired, the Mercer Curriculum Project. (The group dealt with transforming the curriculum in terms of diversity and creating an inclusive classroom atmosphere.) I include these guidelines here as well, along with an example of a written statement that makes classroom behavioral expectations clear. I have highlighted in bold some additions I've made to the document since the publication of *Successful Beginnings* in 2001. Many of my colleagues distribute this sheet to the students in their classes. Others adapt it in some way that better suits their classes and their values. Please feel free to use this tool in any way that works for you.

GUIDELINES FOR COURTESY AND RESPECT:

I would like to welcome all students into an environment that creates a sense of community, pride, courtesy, and respect; we are all here to work cooperatively and to learn together.

In order to create a smooth and harmonious learning community, please make every attempt to come to all the class sessions, to come to class on time, and to stay until the end of the meeting unless you have informed me that you must leave early. There may be a time when you are unavoidably late for class. In that case, please come into the room quietly and choose a seat closest to the entrance. Please see me after class to record your lateness; otherwise you will be marked absent. (Please note that two latenesses to class will be considered the equivalent of one absence, and that poor attendance to class may result in a 10-point penalty, a letter-grade penalty, or withdrawal from the course—see the syllabus for details.)

Please turn off all cell phones and beepers prior to class unless you have informed me that you are, for example, an EMT or a firefighter, **the parent of a young child that you must be available for**, or that you are waiting for a personal emergency call. **If you are expecting a call, please keep your phone on the vibrate mode and step outside to take the call. Otherwise please put your cell phones away at the start of class and keep them away during the entire class period.**

Once the class session has begun, please do not leave the room and then re-enter unless it is an emergency. If you miss a class meeting for any reason, you are responsible for all material covered, for announcements made in your absence, and for acquiring any materials that may have been distributed in class.

It is important that we are all able to stay focused on the class lecture/discussion. For this reason, only one person at a time in the class should be speaking. Side conversations are distracting for surrounding students and for me. As you can see, simple norms of courtesy should be sufficient to have our class run in the best interests of all of us. Thank you in advance for your cooperation.

In my first-day classes, I distributed this guidelines sheet and asked students to read it carefully at home. I discussed some of the key points on the sheet in class and shared my rationale for using such a tool. I told my students that the handout was not etched in stone and that I was open to their feedback. In the next class, I asked if there were any modifications anyone would like to make. No one ever suggested any changes.

As you develop a statement of expectations for your syllabus, or as you create a separate "student conduct guidelines" sheet, it's important that you set a tone of fostering a positive, welcoming classroom climate. Your guidelines should reflect the idea that you're in charge of the classroom dynamic, but they shouldn't sound authoritarian. Remember: An authoritarian tone, whether in your handouts or in how you present yourself, is a sure-fire way to stir some students' rebelliousness and hostilities.

Chismark et al. (2005) also emphasize the importance of making your expectations clear, and they offer some tips related to the course syllabus. These educators say that we as teachers should explain the purpose of the syllabus and incorporate its use throughout the semester. They suggest that we word the syllabus in a professional (not personal) tone. I was pleased to see their emphasis on positive wording of the syllabus. In other words, write your syllabus so that it highlights what your students need to *do* and how they *should* behave to be successful in the course instead of giving them a list of "do nots."

Chismark et al. (2005) stress that your syllabus should have a disclaimer that leaves open the possibility for changes as the semester unfolds. Obviously, you should make adjustments very sparingly and only after careful consideration. Without such a disclaimer, though, students may become quite hostile if/when you must make a change. Given that many of today's students see themselves as consumers, we as teachers need to set realistic goals and have realistic expectations for the course, for our students, and for how our students will be evaluated. If you do make changes to your syllabus, be sure to explain your rationale and to offer reasons that relate to the course subject matter rather than student performance.

Many of us in academia provide "rubrics" for student evaluation—guidelines that spell out what a student needs to accomplish in order to earn a particular grade. As is the case for your syllabus, you need to write your rubrics in positive language and spell out the distinctions between letter grades so that your students can work toward success on an assignment instead of trying to avoid pitfalls.

Chismark and her colleagues (2005) also recommend setting high standards, striving for consistency, and repeating important course policies at strategic points during the semester. In my classes, for example, I would always remind students of the college's academic integrity policy prior to exams and the submission of papers.

Some of my colleagues have recently begun asking their students to create their own behavioral guidelines sheets. These teachers ask groups of four students to work collaboratively to reach consensus on behavioral guidelines for the class. Students are most often willing participants in this exercise, and they tend to create rules that are more stringent than the ones I suggest in my "Guidelines for Courtesy and Respect" handout. Other colleagues of mine ask for student input and work with students—in class—to create the guidelines collectively. Still other colleagues create contracts or

participate in the creation of contracts; the students then
＿ts at the beginning of the term.

Richardson (2000) stresses how important it is for us as teachers to model the mature adult role for our students. He calls today's traditional-age students—those we would refer to as Millennials—"apprentice" adults who are not fully mature. What Richardson said in 2000 holds even more credibility today as we deal with the new, more pampered and protected Millennial student. Richardson (2000, 7) suggests several guidelines that will help you model appropriate classroom behavior:

- Make your behavioral expectations clear in your syllabus. Use positive, constructive language, not threats of reprisal.

- Talk about yourself. Let your students hear what you value.

- Learn about your students. Ask about their hopes and dreams.

- Earn trust by being trustworthy. Live up to your own expectations, and be consistent in applying them to students.

- Prepare your students for active learning by encouraging them to see learning as a process, not a product.

- Use collaborative projects and group dialogue to help your students set and meet expectations for themselves.

- Model adult behavior. Remember that "apprentice" adults take many of their tacit cues from respected mentors.

- Be alert for symptoms of mismatched expectations. Don't ignore even minor incivility; treat it as a sign that expectations need to be realigned.

- Be prepared to adjust your own behavior, if necessary, and to let students learn from your example.

- Take time to discuss your expectations with other teachers. The faculty development center on your campus may sponsor seminars or informal opportunities to learn how other teachers approach civility issues in their classrooms.

chapter, I mentioned how critical it is for us as teachers
＿ime so that we model appropriate classroom behavior. If your schedule permits, it's actually a good idea to get to class early so you can greet your students in a friendly way. Learn your students' names, learn to pronounce their names correctly, and ask them non-invasive questions about themselves. In doing so, you'll form a connection and build rapport. In my research with my own students over the years—and from what I've read about students' preferences—I've discovered that it is extremely important

to most of our students that we know their names and care about them as learners and as people.

Chismark et al. (2005, 10) offer one additional piece of practical advice that could help us all deal more effectively with our students: "Do not take uncivil behaviors personally." Remember when I discussed the baggage that your students might bring to class? Some students experience problems ranging from clinical depression to poor stress management skills and beyond. Other students have unrealistic expectations for themselves and our courses. Often, students project these struggles onto the people around them—including their teachers. So don't be surprised if you get caught in the crossfire at times. If you can step back and disentangle your own ego from the situation, you'll be in a much better position to respond to your students in a mature way.

The importance of respect

An extremely effective deterrent to student incivility is to show your students the respect you hope they'll show you and their classmates. This is yet another way you can role model adult behavior and set the tone for your class. We as instructors are very influential in impacting the class dynamic. If we're able to treat all students with respect, we'll likely reap the benefits.

As I discussed in *Successful Beginnings for College Teaching* (McGlynn 2001), we need to treat our students' *questions* and *comments* in class with respect as well. Even if what our students say is sometimes ignorant, we need to find respectful ways to reframe their comments/questions for the class. That way, we don't accept misinformation as true but we don't embarrass the student either. If students ask questions or make comments that can be construed as sexist, racist, or homophobic, we must view the opportunity as a "teachable moment." Sometimes, when I've been silent after such a statement—probably because I wasn't quick enough to respond—another student in the class has stepped in and handled the situation masterfully. At other times, I have attempted to clarify the issue without in any way accusing the student of prejudice.

If we diminish a student's self-esteem—unintentionally or, much worse, on purpose—we not only reduce the chances of that student participating in the future, we also lessen the likelihood that other students will ask or answer questions. One of the major themes of Amada's (1999) book centers on the issue of respect. There must be a collegial sense of respect throughout the institution: respect for staff, faculty, administrators, and—especially—students. Amada also stresses that we as teachers must be on the same page as administrators when it comes to responding to disruptive behavior among students. A mechanism should be in place for the clear and concise documentation of problems, and there should be a timely, appropriate administrative response to classroom incidents involving incivility. The institution should have clear policies about what constitutes violation of classroom and campus civility, not to mention what the consequences of such behavior are. All of this critical information should be displayed prominently in the institution's student handbook.

Disruptive classroom behaviors and how best to manage them

Even in classes where teachers model appropriate behavior, respect their students, make their academic and behavioral expectations clear, and create an inclusive, welcoming environment, managing the classroom itself can still be a challenge.

At the beginning of this chapter, I mentioned the difficulty of using the ambiguous term "incivility." Although we might not have a clear definition of the concept, I think most of us recognize behaviors that don't belong in the college classroom. Indeed, I think most college instructors would agree that the following student behaviors can be problematic:

- Talking while the instructor or another student is speaking. Carrying on side conversations is disruptive not only for the teacher but for other students as well.
- Monopolizing the class discussion.
- "Stalking" the professor. When I use the term "stalking" in this context, I'm not referring to serious cases where students actually harass professors in a threatening way. I'm referring to the more benign behavior of students following their professors around, craving their attention.
- Allowing their cell phones to ring during class. Some students even answer their calls while class is going on or step out to take a call.
- Using a cell phone during class to send or receive text messages, listen to voice mail, look at photos, or play games.
- Using laptops in class—not to take notes but to e-mail/Instant Message and to play games.
- Wearing headphones in class to listen to music.
- Passing notes to other students or playing games.

- Reading newspapers or magazines, or doing other non-related schoolwork.
- Doodling in a notebook, doing crossword puzzles, or sleeping.
- Being consistently late.
- Walking into class late and passing in front of the instructor.
- Walking in and out of class for no apparent good reason.
- Exhibiting disruptive behavior in a large-lecture setting—for instance, carrying on a side conversation or walking out of the lecture hall and then back in.
- Showing disrespect for their classmates or the teacher by tone of voice, body language, or any behavior that most people would consider insolent, challenging, threatening, or in any way intimidating.
- Misusing the professor's telephone or e-mail availability.
- Violating the rules of academic integrity by cheating on exams and/or plagiarizing their papers.

The Side Conversationalists

Your behavioral guidelines sheet should have wording that addresses behavioral issues in a positive way. For example, you might include something similar to the last paragraph of the "Guidelines for Courtesy and Respect" handout I highlighted earlier. In other words, put in writing something about your desire to promote an atmosphere that is conducive to courteous classroom discussion. You can then refer to that guideline if students aren't abiding by it. For instance, if students were engaged in side conversations while I was speaking or one of their classmates had the floor, I would stop and say, "Please remember that only one person should be talking at a time." If a group of students was speaking on top of another student's statement, I would say, "In this course, we would like to hear everyone's ideas."

In *Successful Beginnings for College Teaching* (McGlynn 2001, 108-109), I addressed the many ways we can deal with students who carry on side conversations with their classmates during class:

> For many students who talk to the people next to them, simply looking at them—that is, making direct eye contact—stops their talking. Sometimes, walking toward them and looking at them stops their talking. On occasion, though, I've had students who seem not to be able to stop themselves from talking in class even

when I look at them. With students I have felt comfortable with, I've put my hand on their shoulder while I continue to discuss the material. This has always stopped their conversation abruptly. However, it's important for you to have established rapport with the student before trying this strategy; otherwise, the student may simply feel intimidated, and you may lose him or her.

You might also try directing a question to someone who is sitting close to the person who's talking. If you ask the student who is talking to answer a question, not only might you turn that student off to you and the class, but you may also turn off other students as well. The classroom atmosphere should feel safe. Asking a student a question when you know he or she isn't paying attention is perceived as a threat. Asking a nearby student to answer a question is a better solution because it focuses the class attention to the part of the room where the disruption is and will likely "nudge" the disrupter(s) to stop talking.

If the various in-class strategies you try don't work, talk to the disrupter(s) privately before or after class. You can catch the talkers on the way out of the room, for example, and say, "May I speak with you for a minute?" You can then explain how their talking during class is distracting to you and to the other students. You can ask the students to hold their conversations outside of class. With students who seem not to be able to stop talking to their friends, you can ask that they take seats far enough away from each other so that they're not tempted. You can say this lightheartedly and maybe with humor so as not to alienate them. Students are generally much more cooperative if they feel you understand their behavior but simply cannot condone it. If you take a hard-line attitude with them, you may get them to stop talking in your class—but you may also encourage them to stop attending class altogether, or to let their minds wander when they do show up.

A variation on casually asking students who are on their way in or out of class to speak with them is to call their names during class (when they're talking) and tell them you'd like to speak with them after class. This approach generally stops the student from talking for the rest of the session but it definitely has its risks. Everyone in the class now knows that the student will be reprimanded in some way. You haven't actually reprimanded the student in front of the class, but by calling the student's name, you've highlighted his or her misbehavior. The advantage of this strategy is that the entire class will probably be quiet for the class hour. The disadvantage is that you may have effectively stifled some appropriate class interaction by playing the "authority" role. The student you asked to speak with may feel embarrassed, threatened, and even hostile toward you. Despite the potential drawbacks, you may be forced to use this strategy in some circumstances. However, try alternative approaches first, since the ideal is to win the person, not the point.

The Class "Monopolizers"

We've all had to deal with the class "monopolizer" at one time or another. These students have also been referred to as "compulsive communicators." Munde (2002) and Fortney et al. (2001) define compulsive communicators as students who dominate classroom discussion. These students consistently communicate in class more than their peers do, and they often seem unaware of the potentially negative impact they're having on their teachers and classmates.

Fortney et al. (2001) found that compulsive communicators may cause other students to withdraw from participating in class. Those who do withdraw, according to Fortney and his colleagues, see the more frequent talkers as more competent (even though this is often not the case) and see themselves as less competent by comparison. There are also students who see the compulsive communicators as know-it-alls and obnoxious. These students sometimes roll their eyes or make disruptive noises when the monopolizer speaks. All in all, compulsive talkers can create an atmosphere that is not conducive to the best interests of the whole class.

Fortney et al. (2001) suggest structuring group activities that limit the compulsive talker's role within the group so that he or she doesn't dominate. For example, you might assign specific roles to group members and give fewer verbal roles (e.g., timekeeper, group recorder) to the compulsive talker.

Several other strategies can also be effective. Since compulsive talkers are often negative attention seekers, you could give the person some attention at the break or before or after class. You could also politely cut the monopolizer off during class with a remark such as, "That's a very interesting point. Let's hear what other people think." You can acknowledge the question or comment but give limited time to it and move on. You can also build up the compulsive talker's self-esteem with a comment such as, "We know you know the answer but let's give someone else a turn." Chismark and her colleagues (2005) suggest trying to compliment compulsive talkers by saying things like, "You're ahead of me; we'll get to that shortly," or "I can tell you've given this some thought," or "Does anyone else have some thoughts on this issue?"

You can also try to avoid eye contact with the monopolizer. And if he or she blurts something out, you can remind the class as a whole about the importance of raising one's hand to contribute. You can also establish eye contact with people on the other side of the room and, with your body language, exclude the monopolizer. If the compulsive talker rambles away from the subject, you can refocus the class's attention by restating the relevant point. You can direct questions to the class that are back on topic. You can change course by writing on the board, flipping on the overhead projector, or moving on to the next slide of your PowerPoint presentation.

What has worked for me when all else fails is to engage the student after class in a discussion about his or her participation. You can phrase your request in a positive way: "I'm happy to see that you're so involved in the course material, but I would like to get the students who take longer to put their thoughts together into the conversation. The only way that will happen is if you can be quiet and we can both give them the opportunity to participate."

The "Stalkers"

Some students follow us around outside of class. They frequent our office hours and tag along with us from classroom to classroom, seemingly in constant need of our attention. In many cases, these are needy students who might do well to see a student development staff member for personal counseling. It's important—for us and for them—that we set limits and boundaries, and that we do so in a humanistic way. You can tell the "stalkers" the parameters of your time with them: "I can speak with you for a few minutes and then I have a meeting to attend," or "I'd like to talk further with you but I have all this work to get done today." In some instances, when students weren't responsive to these types of remarks or to my body language, I'd get up and ask them to walk with me to the main division office—where I would then "get busy"—or I'd ask them to walk with me to my next meeting. If we're clear about our expectations, students usually catch on.

In a few cases, students develop romantic attachments to their professors and follow them around endlessly. Once again, it's important for you to set limits and boundaries. In fact, it's imperative. Always speak with these students in a public place or in your office with the door open. I'm less concerned that you'll be "hit on"—to use my Millennial students' vernacular; I'm more concerned that you could be accused of an impropriety. Some students, when a teacher rejects their ardor, make false accusations about the object of their obsession. If you believe you must say something to the student regarding his or her persistence toward your time and attention, explain that college policy prohibits relationships between faculty and the students in their classes. Document your dealings with such students and keep your department chair or dean in the loop.

Cell Phones in Class

A number of disturbing issues emerge from students' use of cell phones. One way to calm ourselves down about the cell phone issue is to recognize that many of today's students—particularly the Millennials—are incredibly attached to their cell phones. As a Baby Boomer myself, I still marvel at the idea that we can carry around a wireless phone. But for many of our younger students, cell phones are such a part of their lives that it seems as if the cell phone is a part of their anatomy. One of my colleagues shared with me that her 10-year-old son was insisting he "needed" a cell phone. When she asked him why, he replied, "What if I need to get in touch with you?" I laughed at her response to her son: "Why would you worry? You're always under adult supervision."

I introduce this topic this way because I can see that many of us have become a bit "crazy" over the cell phone issue. One way to ease our upset is to frame cell phone behavior as a nuisance—perhaps the way we viewed students chewing gum in class decades ago. I offer this perspective not to suggest that you implement a lenient cell phone policy, but rather to help you avoid getting in a lather about it. Your cell phone policy could read something like the one in the "Guidelines for Courtesy and Respect" I wrote about earlier:

> Please turn off all cell phones and beepers prior to class unless you've informed me that you are, for example, an EMT or a firefighter, the parent of a young child that you must be available for, or that you are waiting for a personal emergency call. If you are expecting a call, please keep your phone on the vibrate mode and step outside to take the call. Otherwise, please put your cell phones away at the start of class and keep them away during the entire class time.

Usually this type of policy does the trick when it comes to students receiving or making calls during class time. If students abuse the policy, I speak to them privately after class.

Unfortunately, there are other cell phone issues apart from students using the phone as a phone. Cell phones are now:

- Cameras
- Vehicles for text messaging
- Vehicles for checking voice mails and e-mails
- Vehicles for storing, viewing, and sending photographs
- Vehicles for connecting to the Internet
- Vehicles for games.

Again, it's important for all of us to develop a little understanding before we create and implement a policy. The traditional-age students of today are the most connected and social of *all* the generations. They interact via cyberspace, and they're in constant communication. It's no wonder they walk into our classes and leave our classrooms talking on the phone or text messaging. The problem arises when they use the phone *during* our classes. There is a simple solution to the many misuses of cell phones during class time: Part of your guidelines sheet must include what I stated earlier: "Please put all cell phones away at the start of class and keep them away during the entire class period." Students may need verbal reminders of this guideline throughout the semester.

USING LAPTOPS IN CLASS—NOT TO TAKE NOTES BUT TO E-MAIL/INSTANT MESSAGE AND TO PLAY GAMES

It can be frustrating when you discover that students who are "working" on their laptops in class are in fact not working at all. We thought that portable notebook computers would revolutionize note taking in class, increasing the amount of information students could record and allowing them to easily make revisions and embellishments after class. Some students are doing just that. But a few are using their laptops to check their e-mail, send Instant Messages, and play games!

Is this yet another example of technology in the service of education gone awry? What can we do to prevent the misuse of laptops in class?

- Ban them altogether—although this is a bit harsh since some students are using them legitimately.
- Make very clear our expectations on how laptops are to be used in class.
- Include in our behavioral guidelines what the consequences are for misuse of laptops in class (e.g., loss of points toward grades).
- Walk around the room frequently and look at what students are doing on their laptops—walking around the room is a good teaching strategy anyway, as it helps keep students engaged.

OTHER DISRUPTIVE BEHAVIOR

This group of behaviors includes wearing headphones in class to listen to music, passing notes to other students, playing games, reading newspapers or magazines, doing other non-related schoolwork, doodling in a notebook, doing crossword puzzles, or sleeping. I've deliberately grouped all of these behaviors into one category because they could all be signs of a student's disengagement with the class. As I discussed in *Successful Beginnings for College Teaching* (McGlynn 2001, 109-110):

> It's tempting to ignore students who sleep in your class, or who do other work clearly not related to your class, because their actions may lower your self-esteem, and/or you simply don't know how to deal with the problem. In the past, whenever I had a student fall asleep in class—and there have been more than a few in my thirty *(now thirty-five!)* years of college teaching—I used to feel somehow responsible for the student's behavior. I often believed that I put the student to sleep by conducting such a boring class. I also felt embarrassed that other students had noticed the sleeper and seen I hadn't responded in any way.

> I no longer ignore sleepers—and neither should you, because chances are their fatigue has nothing to do with you and your teaching performance. Talk to the student who falls asleep in your class. When I've spoken to such students, I've often discovered people who have been carrying incredible work loads, many times coming to class straight from working a shift without sleeping. Talking to students about their schedules and commitments—sometimes their overcommitments—can often be helpful to them.

> They may be able to figure out ways to come to class less exhausted. Additionally, I have on occasion discovered that a sleepy student was on medication for some serious physical problem. In these cases, the student's fatigue has simply been a side effect of the medication. I mention these examples because we're often prone to suspect the worst—of our students and of our own teaching. If we seek and understand the real reasons for a student sleeping in class—instead of falling into the trap of "taking it personally"—we can deal with the issue more effectively.

Students who do other course work in your class are a different matter. Clearly they are disengaged from your teaching efforts.

You need to stop this behavior, because it is not in the student's best interest to "miss" your class, and the other students need to know that the behavior is unacceptable. There are several ways to deal with the student who does unrelated work in your class (or who reads the newspaper or a magazine—yes, it does happen!). Some suggestions:

- Try direct eye contact as you move in the student's direction.
- Ask a neighboring student to answer a question.
- Ask the student who is disengaged to answer a question. *(Note the potential disadvantages of this approach, which I highlighted earlier in this chapter when discussing students engaged in side conversations.)*
- Ask all students to write a response to a question you pose.
- Break the class into pairs or groups and require them to complete a task.
- Speak to the student after class.

The key is to do *something* in these situations! It may be easier (in the short term) to ignore a student's troublesome behavior, but in the end you'll do a disservice to both the student and the class by failing to act. Amada (1999) uses the term *benign neglect* to refer to the strategy of ignoring disruptive behavior in the hopes that it will go away. Some instructors believe that ignoring certain behaviors is a way to avoid reinforcing them, thus ensuring that the behaviors will cease. Amada, however, argues that there are so many other reinforcers of the student's behavior that are outside of our control that the behavior is more likely to continue if we don't intervene.

Being Consistently Late for Class

Students who are frequently late for class can be terribly annoying to any conscientious teacher. First of all, these students often miss important announcements and handouts and interrupt the flow of the class session. If you're in the middle of explaining a concept and then a student walks in late, everyone is distracted—including you. If the class is in the middle of group work, the group the latecomer joins loses valuable time filling that student in on what has occurred so far.

I understand that students may be unavoidably late, particularly at commuter colleges. I'm referring here to students who are *consistently* late. Because consistent lateness is a detriment to both the late student and the rest of us, I instituted a late-to-class policy. I tell students that while I know lateness might be unavoidable, if they're late for class twice they'll be treated as having missed a class—which then may result in a point reduction from the final point total that contributes to their final grade. Both my attendance policy (which involves a possible point reduction) and my lateness-to-class policy are highlighted on my syllabus using the word "may"—i.e., that missing class or being late too often *may* result in a five- or ten-point reduction of points, depending on the number of missed classes." The actual wording is more specific. Here's an example from one of my syllabi in which I use a point system:

> ATTENDANCE POLICY: If you miss the equivalent of one week's classes, your final grade may be lowered by five (5) points. If you miss the equivalent of two weeks' classes, your final grade may be lowered by ten (10) points or a letter grade. If you miss more than the equivalent of two weeks' classes, you may be withdrawn from the course. If you miss more than three class hours, please inform the instructor of your absence so that you will not be withdrawn. If you miss *any* class, please be responsible to get class notes, handouts, etc. (It may help to have available telephone numbers of one or two classmates).

> LATE POLICY: If you arrive to class after attendance has been taken, please take a seat near the entrance and see me after class so I can change your absence to a lateness. Two (2) latenesses equal one absence. If you are able to attend every class throughout the semester, you will receive *five bonus points* added to your total number of points. If you have one excused absence, you will receive *three bonus points*. Remember: If you voluntarily withdraw from any course prior to the 10-week withdrawal deadline, you must fill out the appropriate forms so as not to receive an F (failure) for that course.

Notice two things here. First, I use the word "may" rather than "will" lose points in case there are situations in which I wouldn't want to penalize a student. I tell students, for example, that if they become ill (and the illness is verified) and they must miss class even for two weeks, I won't withdraw them or lower their final grade if they keep up with the work and stay in touch with me.

The second strategy I use is the carrot/stick approach. I offer students bonus points for perfect or near-perfect attendance to motivate them to come to class and be on time. You'd be surprised how many students strive for those few extra points, even though in the big scheme of things they have very little to do with one's final grade. In addition to giving out bonus points for perfect attendance, I buy certificates at the dollar store, insert students' names, sign them (sometimes I get an administrator to sign them too —e.g., the dean of liberal arts or the vice president for academic affairs), and then award them to the students with perfect attendance during the last class session. The other students clap spontaneously, without any push on my part.

If, during the semester, there are students who are consistently late despite my policies, I ask to speak with them privately. I respectfully ask why they have such difficulty getting to class on time. I sometimes discover that they're the sole caretakers of sick parents or children, or that they have some other very legitimate reason for their lateness. Usually, though, these students are the conscientious ones who initiate contact with me after I describe my policy at the beginning of the term.

Here's a response I've heard more often than I care to: "I'm just a late person. I'm late for everything. That is just who I am." One student actually told me that she's usually late for class because no one seemed to care. She told me I was the first professor who had called her on her behavior. (I find this a bit hard to believe but who knows?) In cases where students self-identify as latecomers, I deliver a values talk about the importance of promptness. I tell these students that I'm concerned about their academic success as well as their future success in the workforce, and that their tardiness will not serve them well in either venue. I also suggest simple solutions for their lateness—and every once in a while, a student who has been a consistent latecomer turns things around. I once used a technique I learned from one of my colleagues: I asked the student what time she left the house to get to the college for our class, and how long it usually took her to drive and find a parking spot. This was a student who was consistently twenty minutes late for class. When I got all the information, I suggested that she make a big effort to leave her home twenty minutes earlier. Lo and behold, she started coming to class either on time or at least not as late as she had been showing up.

Walking in Late to Class and Passing in Front of the Instructor
Walking in and out of Class for No Apparent Good Reason

I believe that both of these behaviors are the result of ignorance rather than deliberate rudeness, particularly for Gen Xers and Millennials. Somehow, these students never learned the etiquette of the classroom. Students are often quite surprised when I suggest that no one should leave class and re-enter unless it's an emergency. They usually believe they have the right to do so. I try to lighten the atmosphere by saying something along the lines of, "Please, if you feel you're about to vomit, you may certainly leave class and come back when you're feeling better." I also add, "If you must leave early from class, please inform me before the start of the class."

Walking into class late and in front of the instructor is, in my mind, another example of Millennial obliviousness. I avoid this problem by suggesting to students at the beginning of the semester that they keep the first row of desks closest to the room's entrance empty for people who are unavoidably late to class.

Disruptive Behavior in Large-Lecture Settings

This is another topic I covered in *Successful Beginnings for College Teaching* (McGlynn 2001, 111-112):

> Side conversations among students are much more common in large-lecture situations than in smaller classrooms. ... [T]he greater anonymity students experience in the large lecture setting may encourage some of them to behave in ways they ordinarily would not. I've found, for example, that students who would never talk in a small group feel much freer to talk during large lecture (especially if they're sitting where most talkers tend to sit—in the back rows of the lecture hall). I've also learned that the best way to stop disruptive behavior in large lecture is to try to break down students' sense of "deindividuation." I should mention, though, that I haven't been as successful as I would like to be in this regard: I still have to deal with talkers every semester, but I do find that I'm able to stop the talking patterns earlier in the term, and I feel as if I'm in more control of the class than I was twenty years ago.
>
> I use several strategies to mitigate students' feelings of anonymity in large lecture. In the first class, I explain the attendance policy (which has become more structured over the years). I ask the students to come to class early for the next class period so that they can each select a seat they will keep for the semester. (I tell them that most people automatically sit in the same area anyway, since we're all such creatures of habit.) I also tell them that, according to some research, students tend to do better if they sit close to the front of the room, because they then tend to stay more involved in the class. I note that if students have a strong preference for an aisle seat, they should come early to class for the next session so that they'll be assured of getting one. (I mention this because I've

had several students, more in very recent years, who suffer from panic or anxiety disorders. They want to feel they can leave the room quickly if they have to.) I also tell students that first day that I will try to learn all of their names very quickly.

In the next class session, I have students choose their permanent seats, using a straightforward, fast technique devised by one of my colleagues. Then, for the first couple of weeks in large lecture, I sometimes use a student's name by surreptitiously referring to some sheets in front of me, on which I have students' names and row and seat numbers. I also meet the students once a week in twenty-person seminar classes, where I use additional strategies to memorize their names. Soon, I know enough names to create a large-lecture atmosphere where students feel I know who they are and whether they're there or not. Then, whenever possible, I use a student's name to answer a question, address a comment, or illustrate a point using an example.

In the first lectures of the term, I tell students that, considering the size of the class, it's very important to me that they pay attention and not engage in side conversations. I acknowledge that it is understandable for them to be tempted to talk to a friend in the next seat, but that this behavior cannot be tolerated. I tell them I find side conversations extremely distracting, and that students have complained to me over the years that they too are very distracted by people who talk in class. I remind the students that they are *all* paying tuition to hear these lectures, and that it's part of my role to protect everyone's right to avoid unnecessary distractions.

I've found that the large-lecture atmosphere has to be somewhat different from that of smaller classroom sections. I play much more of an "authority" role in large lecture. I tell students that if they talk with people around them, I will call them by name—and that if I have to call them by name a second time, I'll ask them to leave the lecture hall. I warn the students that I may ask persistent talkers to withdraw from the course. (Note: I make this somewhat authoritarian-sounding statement in the first or second lecture just so students know that I'm serious about not tolerating side conversations. I very rarely use a student's name in this way in large lecture, and then only in extreme cases of disruption. If ever I do use this strategy, it's usually later in the term. By that time I've balanced this hardline position, which may put students off, by building rapport in the smaller seminar classes.)

Unfortunately, some disruptive behavior in large-lecture classes is almost inevitable, unless you're teaching groups of highly motivated, conscientious students. Part of the problem with my introductory psychology large-lecture course is that most students take it freshman year, before they've been socialized as college students. In my experience, students mature as people and as students in their first college year. By their second year, in my advanced courses, students' behavior is much more mature.

There are many techniques I use in large lecture to keep students engaged. ... Obviously, one way to keep disruptive behavior to a minimum is to make the class interesting and to use active learning strategies within the lecture format. I have an edge in that most students *elect* to take courses in my discipline, psychology, and so they're at least somewhat inherently interested in the subject matter.

I will discuss active engagement techniques that are especially useful for the large-lecture format in Chapter 4.

OTHER DISRESPECTFUL BEHAVIOR

These behaviors include: showing disrespect for classmates or the teacher by tone of voice, body language, or behavior that most people would consider insolent, challenging, threatening, or in any way intimidating.

Here's where it helps to have some psychological savvy about people and relationships. Chismark et al. (2005) offer several suggestions for dealing with student anger that may be manifested toward you and/or the other students in the class; much of what I include here is based on their work.

The best ways to defuse anger involve showing empathy toward angry students, acknowledging their feelings, and listening reflectively to what they have to say. When students are confrontational, they're often fearful, frustrated, and/or not managing stress well. If you're able to depersonalize students' anger—it's usually not about *you*—you'll be able to respond empathetically. You won't become angry or defensive yourself, and you thus won't communicate anger or defensiveness verbally or through your body language. You're the professional. It's never appropriate to respond to disrespectful behavior with disrespect. Your role is to model appropriate, civil behavior. You need to maintain a sense of calm to help the student work through his or her issues. Very often what students need is simply a sounding board for their frustrations. If you listen carefully to what they're saying, reflect it back to them, and accept their feelings, you may be surprised that their anger dissipates quickly.

You can show your empathy through active listening, maintaining eye contact with the student, and having an open posture. Chismark et al. (2005) suggest that you let students know you support them. Tell them you want them to be successful in the course. Listen carefully to what they say, and show you understand their position and their frustration even if you don't necessarily agree with it. Chismark et al. further suggest that once you've aligned yourself with angry students, you should restate your position and ask them to consider that position.

If students appear angry, ask them exactly what they're upset about. Then, elicit from them solutions to their problem that would be fair to everyone involved, including the rest of their classmates. You might do some problem solving with such students about policies and accommodations that either you or the college administration has in place that might help them. Give students a way out so that they don't lose face. Don't create a win/lose situation.

If an incident happens with an angry student in the classroom itself, suggest to the student that the two of you discuss the issue after class. If the student leaves in a huff, reassure the rest of the students that you will not allow their learning environment to be compromised. If the angry student stays in the classroom and continues to be belligerent, tell the student that he or she will have to leave the classroom and that you'll speak with him or her privately later. If the student continues to disrupt the class and simply will not leave, be sure you're familiar with your institution's policy about having a student removed from class. At many colleges and universities, the teacher can call security and have a student removed. With documentation of a serious incident, teachers usually have the right to have disruptive students removed from a course permanently. Know the procedures your institution has in place. Talk to other faculty members about how they've handled similar situations. Hopefully, you'll be able to defuse the student's anger before it becomes a serious incident.

When you do speak to the student in question, do so out of earshot of his or her classmates. But don't have the conversation in an isolated place. Be sure to keep your own safety foremost in your mind.

MISUSING THE PROFESSOR'S TELEPHONE OR E-MAIL AVAILABILITY

In *NISOD Innovation Abstracts*, professor of social sciences Jerry Clavner (2006) offers suggestions for creating a positive communication atmosphere regarding telephone and e-mail messages between students and teachers. Once again, the key is to *prevent* telephone and/or e-mail communication from becoming uncivil—and again, a guidelines sheet is probably the best way to make your expectations clear.

Instead of presenting Clavner's suggestions here verbatim, I will extrapolate, modify, and tailor them for your possible use.

Besides having your guidelines in print, it helps to leave a clear voice mail message on your college phone so that when students call you they'll know exactly what to do. My college voice mail said something like this:

> You have reached the voice mail of Angela McGlynn. If you would like to leave me a message, please clearly state your full name, which class you are in, the concise message you would like to leave me, and a clearly articulated phone number and the best times for me to reach you. Thank you.

On your guidelines sheet, Clavner suggests, tell students to consult their course syllabus and/or other students to see if they can find the answer to their question before calling or e-mailing you. This is probably good advice for students, but I'm of two minds about it. On the one hand, it may reduce the number of unnecessary contacts we have with our students. Then again, I would hate to dissuade students from feeling free to contact us, since some of them are reluctant to do so in the first place.

Clavner's suggestions for e-mail etiquette are meant to prevent inappropriate or uncivil student-teacher communication in cyberspace. I reproduce here most of Clavner's suggestions with very slight modifications. I would add one thing to the beginning of Clavner's list: the word "please," so as to soften the tone of the guidelines:

- Do not send jokes, smilies, or other superfluous materials.
- Send material in the exact format the teacher requires.
- Make sure your work has identifiers (name, class and section, assignment name and number) in the body of the attachment and not just in the e-mail message.
- Make sure your proper e-mail address is hyperlinked, especially if you're using a library or someone else's computer to send mail.
- Make sure your message and attachments are virus-free.
- Do not rely on spell check; proofread and correct everything before you send it.
- Do not send anything in anger.

- Make sure you type in the recipient's address correctly to ensure receipt. (Clavner 2006)

Epstein (2006) discusses the work of two faculty members at the University of Oregon who have added "netiquette" to their class syllabi. After reading a *New York Times* article about students filling professors' e-mail boxes with questions on where to buy school supplies, critical comments about classmates, and vents about grades, assistant professor of anthropology Lamia Karim added e-mail guidelines to her course syllabus. Basically, Karim tells students not to e-mail her with trifles, not to ask her for information that is already on the syllabus, and to use professional language rather than terms such as "yo." She also asks students to address their professors as "professor" unless told otherwise by the teacher, and she says she'll call students by title as well if they prefer.

Karim's University of Oregon colleague, Sarah McClure, an adjunct assistant professor of anthropology, has also added "netiquette" guidelines to her syllabus. She asks students to talk to her in person before or after class if their question requires more than a single-sentence response or a back-and-forth exchange. She also reminds her students that e-mails are public documents, even if they're sent to someone privately.

Simple suggestions on your course syllabus regarding e-mail and phone communication can prevent most of the problems that can arise.

Violating the Rules of Academic Integrity by Cheating on Exams and/or Plagiarizing Papers

If we believe both the popular media and some scholarly surveys, cheating is rampant among college students. Rebekah Nathan (a pseudonym), a professor of anthropology at a major university, went underground as a student to learn what it's like to *be* a student on today's college campus. In her acclaimed book *My Freshman Year* (Nathan 2005), she discusses the phenomenon of cheating along with a host of other topics. Based on the national data she reviewed, it is undeniable that college students cheat. Nathan says that at least half of college students engage in serious cheating, that more than two-thirds admit to cheating on a test, and that more than 75 percent have cheated in some capacity.

Instead of seeing cheating as an issue of individual morality, Nathan says, we need to examine the role of the undergraduate culture. Interestingly, she notes that although there has been a slight increase in cheating among today's college students—particularly in the electronic realm (e.g., downloading someone else's work from the Internet)—cheating has been prominent since the early days when academics began measuring the phenomenon. As far back as the nineteenth century, cheating was reported as an active part of the college culture. It obviously remains so today.

In her research on cheating, Nathan discovered that most students don't support the idea of cheating when it is understood as consistently gaining unfair advantage over classmates by engaging in dishonest academic behavior. As was the case in the national studies, Nathan also found that students question what constitutes cheating and what's legitimate. They tend to perceive subtleties and nuances with regard to what academic honesty is all about. Many students see ambiguity in the phenomenon of cheating and say the behavior must be examined in context.

Nathan discusses research done at a North Carolina university in which participating students offered reasons they thought should be taken into account in disciplining a student who is caught cheating. Among the reasons Nathan (2005, 126) highlights:

- Performance pressure
- Personal problems that made it difficult or impossible to study
- Unrealistic expectations of instructors
- Meaningless or irrelevant assignments

The national trend in academia is that students are increasingly finding cheating to be more acceptable and justifiable. Donald McCabe and the Center for Academic Integrity have been conducting national studies on academic honesty for more than four decades. In recent years, McCabe (2000) notes, there has been a disturbing shift in students' attitudes toward cheating. In fact, he says, students are able to justify and rationalize their cheating with greater ease today than they did decades ago.

Nathan explains that if we are to understand the cheating rage on college campuses for what it truly is (rather than as simply an example of immorality), we need to understand the role of the institutional culture in impacting people's behavior. This is a social psychological perspective that resonates well with me. From Solomon Asch's classic conformity studies (Asch 1951) to Philip Zimbardo's famous prisoner-guard study at Stanford University (Zimbardo 1970), we have ample research showing that individual behavior is a function of cultural context and other people.

Through her own observational research, Nathan was able to gain some insight into cheating by walking in the shoes of students. What she discovered by living among them is that the national literature is inadequate when it comes to describing issues of academic integrity and dishonesty. She found quite a different picture from that depicted in the literature. She says that some cheating results from competing cultural values rather than lack of morality. For example, most students value honesty but are reluctant to turn in another student for cheating or to decline a classmate's request for help with homework. What she found from a North Carolina university study done in 2001 is that most examples of cheating involve behaviors that value student reciprocity and mutual aid over attending strictly to rules. Some common examples: signing an attendance roster for an absent student, getting questions or answers from other students who have already taken a test, or working on an assignment with other students.

The most common forms of cheating also include making false excuses to buy time for completing an assignment, adding phony bibliographic sources, or copying from a source without footnoting. Although Nathan doesn't condone cheating in college, her review of the literature—and especially her experience living among today's college students—give her a way to understand what it's all about. From her perspective, cheating is a function of the complex aspects of college life—such as too little time to complete one's work, competition for grades, and the perceived irrelevancy of certain assignments.

Another recent study adds to our understanding of the role of cultural pressure on students to succeed. It also supports McCabe's (2000) assertions on the ease with which today's students rationalize their behavior. A *USA Today* "Snapshots" feature (Briggs and Gonzalez 2006) reports on a survey of 36,000 high school students between the ages of fourteen and nineteen. The students came from 114 schools and were questioned between January and June 2006. With a margin of error of only plus or minus one percentage point, the study showed that half of teenage boys and 33 percent of teenage girls believe a person has to lie or cheat sometimes to succeed. The overall percentage for both genders was 42 percent.

Gallant and Drinan (2006) come to conclusions similar to Nathan's in their organizational theory of cheating. They write (841):

> Organizational theory situates the student cheating problem in the context of the educational institution as a complex organization affected by people, time, and social forces.

These researchers and others, such as Senge (1990), suggest that if we really want to understand cheating, we need to look beyond individual patterns of student cheating behaviors to the systemic explanations for those behaviors. In other words, what is it about the college culture that promotes cheating?

The high school survey I just mentioned evokes questions about the impact of the culture preceding college as well. Gallant and Drinan (2006) suggest institutional strategies for colleges and universities that would be aimed less on reducing student cheating and more on the broader goal of institutionalizing academic integrity by creating a community culture that highly values integrity and learning.

Beyond advocating for systemic changes in our institutions, I believe that we as teachers can do more to prevent cheating in the first place. To use a Baby Boomer expression, *this may sound like a broken record*—but having clear expectations about academic integrity and making your expectations known to your students, both verbally and in writing, may help mitigate the incidence of cheating. Most colleges and universities have published policies about academic integrity. Know your own institution's policy and give it to your students—in writing. Discuss the policy at the beginning of the semester and remind students of it before exams and when papers are due. Here's an example of what I included about academic integrity on my own course syllabi (drawn from my college's policy):

> ACADEMIC INTEGRITY: Academic Integrity refers to the "integral" quality of the search for knowledge that a student undertakes. The work a student produces, therefore, ought to be wholly his or hers; it should result completely from the student's own efforts.
>
> A student will be guilty of violating Academic Integrity if he/she: a) uses or obtains unauthorized assistance in any academic work; b) gives fraudulent assistance to another student; c) knowingly represents the work of others as his/her own, or represents previously completed academic work as current; d) fabricates data in support of an academic assignment; and/or e) inappropriately or unethically uses technological means to gain academic advantage.

In discussions about academic integrity in my classes, I would be more specific about the differences between students helping each other and "stealing" the work of others. I would tell them about the legal term *intellectual property* and the serious consequences of violations in the "real world." Long before papers were due, I would give students another handout explaining how to cite references using American Psychological Association (APA) style, and I'd explain how to use the college's electronic databases to find scholarly, peer-reviewed journals.

BBC News (2006) reported that one expert in the assessment field, Professor Sally Brown—pro-vice-chancellor for assessment, learning, and teaching at Leeds Metropolitan University—believes that many students of the new generation who were raised on the Internet see nothing wrong with using other people's work. The Internet has made copying and pasting all too easy, and many "Google Generation" students don't understand what plagiarism is. Brown says the violations among today's students result from poor academic practices, such as not keeping good records of where the material they use comes from and/or not recognizing the concepts of academic ownership and authorship. Brown suggests personalizing assignments to make plagiarism difficult. She suggests "designing an assignment out"—in other words, that we create assignments requiring students to use personal knowledge, keep a journal or diary, and show their progression on the work during the stages toward completion. Indeed, many professors who assign papers create topics that would not be found on the Internet and require students to meet with them periodically to go over their references and early drafts. These types of tailored assignments reduce the possibility that students will buy papers or download other people's work from the Internet.

In *The Teaching Professor*, Ed Johnson (1999) wrote a valuable piece called "Preclude Cheating: A Response." In the article, Johnson challenges the idea that students are the bad guys and poses ways that we as teachers can prevent or mitigate cheating instead of simply being enforcers of the consequences of cheating after the fact. In Johnson's view, establishing teacher-student connections and rapport is the first step. In other words, cheating will be less likely to occur in classes where students feel a bond with the teacher. Teachers who create assignments involving analysis and synthesis and give paper topics that are not easily found on the web will also decrease the likelihood that their students will cheat.

Johnson (1999) also suggests that we involve our students in the evaluation of their own learning; that we give them nonjudgmental feedback on their performance; and that we de-emphasize grades as much as possible. I recognize that de-emphasizing grades is no easy task given that students often think (and are taught to believe) that grades are everything. However, if we can truly engage students in the learning process in a way that gets them excited about *what* they are learning, perhaps it's possible to steer them slightly away from seeing their grade point average as the most important aspect of their education.

Johnson proposes that we redefine the teacher role as mentor, coach, and co-learner rather than as expert. Here's a slight modification of the pedagogical tips Johnson offers (1999, 5) to mitigate cheating among our students:

- Give take-home assignments and open-book exams.
- Encourage cooperative and collaborative learning in groups.
- Tailor assignments to students' strengths and offer flexibility in how they can meet your learning-outcomes goals.

- Get students engaged in meta-cognition tasks in which they explore *how* they know something or *how* they learned something.

In my view, our role as teachers is to help change the institutional climate so that honesty and integrity are highly valued. To do that, we need to convey these values to our students in every class we teach.

In Chapter 4, I discuss strategies to make learning more engaging —another strategy that may reduce the amount of cheating among students.

Teaching to Promote Active Learning, Student Engagement, and Critical Thinking Skills in Today's College Classroom

How can we help today's college students *learn how to learn* so that they become lifelong seekers of knowledge? How can we teach them to think critically and analytically? Can we teach them the ability to discern credible information from unreliable information—the process educators are now calling *information literacy*? How can we teach today's students to write and speak clearly, to learn the content of our courses, and to appreciate diversity in our classes and in our world? The challenges before us may seem overwhelming, but it's imperative that we strive to reach these goals.

Decades of research support the ideas of two pioneers in the field of learning and education. A leading Swiss psychologist, Jean Piaget, studied "thinking and learning" processes by observing his own three children. He eventually discussed the importance of active learning in his classic work *The Origins of Intelligence in Children* (Piaget 1952). Another pioneering work, John Dewey's *Experience and Education* (Dewey 1963), also supported the notion that students learn more effectively when they're actively involved in the learning process. In other words, students learn at deeper levels and retain more of that learning when it involves *doing* something rather than simply receiving information.

Research on learning and memory also shows that the more actively engaged students are in their learning, the deeper their understanding will be and the greater the chance they'll retain their knowledge over time. Certainly the *National Survey of Student Engagement* (NSSE) highlighted in Chapter 2—along with its counterpart for the two-year college sector, the *Community College Survey of Student Engagement* (CCSSE)—have given us additional nationwide data that corroborate this perspective. Indeed, as noted in the 2006 CCSSE Executive Summary, *Act on Fact: Using Data to Improve Student Success* (Community College Survey of Student Engagement 2006, C2):

> Research shows that the more actively engaged students are—
> with college faculty and staff, with other students, and with the
> subject matter they study—the more likely they are to learn, to
> stick with their studies, and to attain their academic goals. Student engagement, therefore, is a valuable yardstick for assessing
> the quality of colleges' educational practices and identifying ways
> they can produce more successful results—more students across
> all subgroups learning at higher levels and attaining their academic goals.

However, although we now have decades of empirical research that supports the work of these early pioneers and these national surveys, many of us as college teachers are reluctant to change our ways (understandably so). Despite research questioning its effectiveness, the lecture mode of educating students still predominates in college classes. College teachers, again understandably, worry about covering the content of their courses, particularly those that serve as foundations for higher-level courses. Many instructors, therefore, use the most efficient way of imparting large quantities of information to their students in the allotted class time: They simply tell their students what they know in their disciplines or areas of expertise. There is a sad truth underneath this reality: As efficient and, in many cases, cost-effective as lecturing may be, it is the *least* effective way for students to learn and retain information.

Do we simply abandon lecturing as a teaching tool? I think not. There will always be a place for explaining theory and concepts and sharing our perspectives on our subjects. But the old format of the fifty- to seventy-five minute lecture no longer works with today's students. It was never the best way to get students actively engaged with the material, but previous generations were more tolerant of the lecture mode. Many of today's students have been raised in what Prensky (2001, 3) calls the "twitch speed" mode of immediate feedback, not to mention the world of hypertext that can take them from one place to another in a non-linear way. The average adult attention span has always been about twenty minutes. But today's students have trouble staying engaged for even that long when we ask them to be passive recipients of information.

The lecture mode needs to change; it needs to become more interactive and engaging.

The interactive lecture

The traditional lecture will still work for some of our students, especially if we happen to be dynamic speakers. For example, the lecture may very well capture—and perhaps even be the preferred mode of instruction for—our older students and our Baby Boomer students. But I doubt the traditional lecture will be the instructional approach of choice for Gen Xers, and it certainly won't be for our Millennial students.

So many lecturers are trying to become more interesting and dynamic—which can certainly help engage students. As I mentioned in *Successful Beginnings for College Teaching* (McGlynn 2001), there are researchers who offer valuable strategies for making traditional lectures more interactive.

Silberman (1996) offers suggestions for getting students' attention at the beginning of a lecture and then maintaining it during the presentation itself. Among Silberman's suggestions (19-21):

- Start your lecture with an interesting story or anecdote that grabs students' attention.
- Begin the lecture with a provocative visual, such as a cartoon.
- Pose a problem or ask a question that is at the center of the lecture so that students will be motivated to stay tuned in.
- Limit the major points of your lecture. Present key terms and concepts on an overhead transparency or whiteboard to help students remember them.
- Use plenty of real-life examples and comparisons, and try to relate your information to your students' previous experiences.
- Wherever possible, use transparencies, flip charts, and handouts to give your students a visual as well as an auditory channel of learning.

- Periodically, stop lecturing so that you can ask students to give examples of the concepts you've presented so far.

- Present a problem or question for students to address based on the information covered in the lecture.

- Toward the end of the lecture, give students a test or quiz on the topic covered. (Note: I don't use this particular technique myself, for fear that students will anxiously focus on details instead of listening to the big picture of the topic. However, colleagues who use the technique have had success with it. They tell students ahead of time that there will be a short quiz at the end of class that asks them to answer questions related to the most important topics covered. The technique motivates some students to stay tuned into class, my colleagues say.)

- Ask students to compare their notes with each other in order to review the lecture and clear up any questions they may have.

The field of acting offers even more ideas on ways we can liven up the traditional lecture. Theater professor Morris Burns of the University of Texas (1999) outlines several such strategies:

- Bring more feeling into your presentation of ideas so that you show enthusiasm for what you're teaching. Being passionate about your subject is the best way to accomplish this objective. If you find yourself less passionate than you were when you began teaching, attend professional development workshops in your discipline so that you may recapture some of enthusiasm.

- Picture yourself successfully conducting your classes. Your imagination will pave the way for solid performance in the classroom.

- Use your voice in ways that are conducive to effective communication. For example, speak with inflection rather than droning on in a monotone.

- Use the way you move in class to project enthusiasm and connect with your students. For example, walk around the classroom and establish eye contact with students as you move.

- Think about the arrangement of your teaching environment. Check out, ahead of time, the room where you'll be teaching. Plan ways you can use the space to its best advantage—for instance, whether you should group students in circles or semicircles.

- Prepare for class by thinking about not only the content you want to present, but also your students as audience members and individuals. Deliver your content in a way that is relevant to your students' lives by using examples they can relate directly to their everyday experiences. This is easy to do in my discipline of psychology, but I've watched teachers in so many other disciplines as well—including mathematics—find ways for students to apply what they learn to their own lives.

Given the short attention span of the typical adult, we must introduce ways to interrupt the lecture and allow for our students to assimilate the material we've covered up to that point. Bonwell and Eison (1991) suggest a two-minute pause after you've lectured for fifteen or twenty minutes. During that pause, you could ask your students to summarize (in writing) the lecture so far.

You could also pose a question suggested by Angelo and Cross (1993) in their "Minute Paper" exercise (148-153): "What was the most important (significant, crucial) thing that you learned in today's class?" Angelo and Cross (1993, 154) also suggest asking students to respond to another question: "What was the muddiest point in _____?" You could fill in the blank with endings such as "in today's class?" or "on the topic of...?"

In my large-lecture classes with 200+ students, I often used the Minute Paper technique to pause my lecture. I had a wireless microphone, so I could move all around the lecture hall. What did I discover? That students' responses to the first question—the one about the most important or significant thing they had learned so far—served as a wonderful way to review the material we had just covered. I would walk all around the room repeating what a particular student had said, often using that student's name to boost his or her self-esteem and make the class feel more intimate. Then, when I asked students to read their responses to the second question—the one about what information was still unclear to them—I had the opportunity to ask other students to clarify the material. I could explain things further if necessary. It was a wonderful spot check that helped me see whether the students were following what I was covering.

Bonwell and Eison (1991) discovered that the pause technique improves students' short- and long-term retention of the course content. They also found that it motivates students to focus on the lecture and take meaningful notes.

Pauses can also be used to ask students questions, collectively, during lectures. Even with large groups of students, you can pepper your lecture with questions that get the students involved in the class. Examples:

- How many of you believe that …?
- How many of you believe that it might be possible to …?
- Where do you stand on the controversial issue of …?

In wired classrooms where students can offer feedback using clickers on their desks, it's now possible to ask these kinds of questions and get the whole class's responses on the front screen. That way, students can see their own responses in relation to the responses of the class as a whole. Students appear to be very engaged with this new technology, which allows them to gather information instantly. It fits into their desire for immediacy, instant feedback, and social connectedness.

In my own large-lecture classes, I sometimes posed content-related questions and asked for volunteers to answer them. Often, I first had the students write their answers down. This tends to get more of them *thinking about the question* and volunteering to respond. Sometimes I asked for several people to respond sequentially to the same question, then had students summarize the common threads in all the answers.

For today's students, visuals are effective in the large-lecture format. A PowerPoint presentation that is well done is an effective pedagogical tool. Combining a PowerPoint with video clips and relevant pieces from the Internet is even more engaging, especially for Millennial students. It always helps to organize your lectures with numerous examples and illustrations that are relevant to your students' lives, and to deliver your lectures with enthusiasm. In my own research with students, the teacher's enthusiasm is always something students see as motivational. Of course, a little humor during class also goes a long way toward engaging your students and building rapport with them.

Bonwell and Eison (1991) also suggest some other ways you can make lectures more interactive. For instance, you can use strategically placed quizzes during the lecture to:

- Engage your students in demonstrating what they've just learned.
- Identify what your students don't yet understand.
- Take the pulse of your students with respect to how effective your lecture has been up to that point.

In addition to the pause technique and the use of quizzes, Bonwell and Eison (1991) discuss what they call the *feedback lecture*, the *guided lecture*, and the *responsive lecture*. The feedback lecture consists of two mini lectures that are interrupted for a problem-solving activity. In the guided lecture, students listen to a mini lecture and then spend five minutes writing as much as they can remember about it. They then form small groups, discuss what they've written, and collectively rewrite their notes. In the responsive lecture, you set aside one lecture a week for student-generated questions and respond to those questions for the entire class period.

The move from content to process

There is a sad truth about being committed to teaching *content:* Not only will students forget most of what they learn when they leave our courses —and indeed most of the content of their degrees within a few years of graduation (unless they use the material on a regular basis)—but the content they do remember will probably become outdated rather quickly. The information explosion and the changing nature of what we "know" in the last couple of decades alone attest to the fact that *what* we teach may be less important than teaching students other skills. I do recognize that some disciplines may have less content change than others. But even subjects like mathematics can, and often do, teach students *how to think* rather than giving them a body of information to memorize.

If our students aren't going to remember what they take in—assuming they *are* learning the information in the first place—then what is the value of a college education apart from the obvious economic advantages of having a degree? What is our role as college teachers if it's not to tell our students what we've learned about our disciplines?

When I was stuck in the *content* mode of teaching—as I was learning more and more in my discipline—I started to feel a bit overwhelmed with what I had to teach in so little time. I'm reminded of the title of Barbara Gordon's 1981 book: *I'm Dancing as Fast as I Can.* I started to feel as if I were *talking* as fast as I could! It took years for me to realize that my job was not necessarily to tell my students everything I knew. Now, don't get me wrong: I didn't abandon the goal of having my students learn the content of my discipline. I simply opened up to some new ideas about *how* to get students to learn, and I expanded my view of what a college education means beyond learning information. I started to see that, as important as the content is, perhaps the learning *process* is at least as critical.

A couple of decades ago, I started to pay more attention to research dealing with newer pedagogies such as collaborative and cooperative learning. I joined an adhoc committee at my college that studied the factors that were important for student retention. I explored what was called "feminist" pedagogy (which should really be called "humanistic" pedagogy)—the research that discussed the role of an inclusive classroom atmosphere and transformation of the curriculum in terms of inclusiveness. I initiated and chaired a committee known as the Mercer Curriculum Project, which had two goals: 1) To transform the curriculum so that our course content was more inclusive; and 2) To help faculty learn how to create a safe, welcoming classroom atmosphere for all students.

I joined my college's Writing across the Disciplines Committee and learned about writing as a teaching and learning tool. I participated on (and later chaired) another grassroots committee known as Master Faculty, which created a time and space for faculty members to gather to discuss teaching. Originally, we paired up and observed each other's classes to learn from one another. We occasionally taught a mini lesson for the whole group. Sometimes we discussed problems we were having with particular student behaviors, and often we discussed teaching strategies. College teaching can be an isolating experience. We can become so overwhelmed with our teaching, advising, and college governance activities that we have little time to talk about teaching.

These grassroots committees that I was a part of—which were not at all related to college governance—had a profound effect on my teaching and my professional development. They helped me understand that teaching is so much more than "covering the content." Working on these committees moved me from focusing almost exclusively on content to examining the process of teaching and learning. I started to realize that it made little sense for me to "cover" the material if students weren't *learning* it. I also started to believe that my job involved the teaching of so many other skills—such as writing, oral communication, and critical thinking—that I would have to find ways to get students to learn my discipline *and* develop these other life-long-learning skills. I especially started reading more about critical thinking skills, trying to determine what they were all about.

Critical thinking:
What is it and how do we foster it?

In addition to teaching students about our disciplines, one of our roles is to help our students develop critical thinking skills. In a webinar I did for Magna Publications—*The Learner-Centered Classroom: Building Rapport and Community* (October 26, 2006)—I discussed the topic of teaching critical thinking skills as part of our mission in academia.

As teachers, advisors, mentors, and facilitators, we must help our students develop the ability to think clearly and critically and to:

- Use reason to solve problems by applying discipline-appropriate methodology and standards.

- Ask informed questions and make informed and evaluative judgments.
- Distinguish between fact and opinion and inferences.
- Understand that "fact" is often a function of perspective.
- Identify and evaluate underlying or implicit assumptions.
- Thoughtfully evaluate diverse perspectives and alternative points of view. (Halstead and Tomson, 2006)

Although there are many definitions of critical thinking, I like the one put forth by Paul and Elder (2006, 4):

> Critical thinking is, in short, self-directed, self-disciplined, self-monitored, and self-corrective thinking. It requires rigorous standards of excellence and mindful command of their use. It entails effective communication and problem-solving abilities and a commitment to overcome our native egocentrism and sociocentrism.

Paul and Elder (2006, 4) also tell us that "critical thinking is the art of analyzing and evaluating thinking with a view to improving it." Similar to Halstead and Tomson, Paul and Elder (2006, 4) suggest that the critical thinker:

- Raises vital questions and problems, formulating them clearly and precisely.
- Gathers and assesses relevant information, using abstract ideas to interpret it effectively.
- Comes to well-reasoned conclusions and solutions, testing them against relevant criteria and standards.
- Thinks open-mindedly within alternative systems of thought, recognizing and assessing, as need be, his or her own assumptions, implications, and practical consequences.
- Communicates effectively with others in figuring out solutions to complex problems.

How can we use the classroom experience to help our students develop critical thinking skills? As I discussed in the webinar, Paul and Elder (2002) suggest that we as instructors ask students to:

- Summarize—in writing and then orally—what the teacher or another student has said.
- Elaborate on what has been said by explaining it in their own words or giving examples.

- Make connections between related concepts.
- Restate in their own words the instructions for an assignment.
- Write down the most pressing question they have up to that point in the class.
- Write down what they consider to be the most confusing point thus far in the class.
- Discuss any of the above with a partner for thirty seconds or a minute, then participate in a group discussion.

Halstead and Tomson (2006) suggest:

- Asking students to deliberate on real-life situations (e.g., having students participate in a mock jury trial).
- Asking students to write and/or orally present persuasive arguments that are based on data and evidence.
- Getting students to debate content-related material.
- Getting students to keep journals on their reactions to and evaluations of what they read for class.
- Creating problem-solving exercises and getting students to work collaboratively.
- Giving students essays to write that ask them to interpret, synthesize, analyze, and evaluate material.

Meta-cognition

To help our students become critical thinkers, it's important for us to guide them through the process of understanding *how they learn* and *how they remember* information. Cognitive psychologists use the term *meta-cognition* to describe these processes.

In the Magna Publications webinar I mentioned previously, I discussed the notion of meta-cognition. Literally, *meta* is a prefix that means "behind" or "hidden." Frederick Ahl, professor of ancient Greek literature at Cornell University, says the prefix *meta* implies the part of something that is not immediately visible but is in the background and still has an effect. When *meta* is attached to the word "cognition"—a term that relates to thinking, learning, and memory—meta-cognition becomes the process by which we step back and analyze *how we think, how we learn,* and *how we remember information.*

Understanding our information processing strategies can be powerfully important in helping us develop effective learning tools for our lifelong learning journey. Teaching our students to learn *how* they learn may be, in many cases, more important than teaching them *what* to learn—i.e., the content of our courses.

I'd like to give you just one example of a meta-cognition exercise I used in class. (This particular exercise could also be used in a U.S. history course, and I can imagine various adaptations for other disciplines as well.) Since I taught psychology, one of the topics I covered in "Introduction to Psychology" was memory. I asked my students to write down the names of as many U.S. presidents as they could remember. I told them the presidents' names didn't need to be in historical order. (Note: If there were international students in the class who had been educated outside the United States, I asked them to choose any other list they may have memorized or that they were very familiar with at one point in their lives).

I then told the students that they should use various strategies to try to remember the presidents, and that if they found themselves stuck they should try a different strategy. I said I would give them a hint: that there have been 43 presidents of the United States, including the present one. Usually, students would laugh at that clue, but my motivation in giving it to them was to urge them to use the laws of recency and primacy in their memory strategies. In other words, I was hoping that some students would start from the current president and go backwards—and that when they got stuck, they would try to remember our earliest presidents.

After a few minutes, I told the students that I wasn't really interested in how many presidents they could remember. I told them I was instead wondering *how* they remembered the names they did. Students often told me that my hint helped, since many of them wouldn't otherwise have started at the end and worked their way backwards before trying to remember the earliest presidents. The students also shared that when they got stuck, they thought of events such as wars, the Great Depression, and assassinations. They also thought of portraits on folded money, pictures they remembered along the borders of their grade school classrooms, and songs they'd learned as youngsters.

The point: They were identifying the strategies they had used to retrieve information from their memory banks. Noticing how the brain works and learning to develop learning and retrieval strategies based on that knowledge can be enormously helpful in the learning process.

"Deep" thinking

Joe Cuseo, whom I mentioned in Chapter 1 for his work with the course syllabus and the "Student Information Sheet," has done extensive work on what he calls "deep thinking." In his work "Questions That Promote Deeper Thinking" (2000), Cuseo says he uses the term "deep thinking" rather than "critical thinking" to avoid the common misperception among students that critical thinking literally means being critical.

Cuseo broadens the usual definitions of critical thinking to include all types of thinking that are deeper than memorization and recall of facts. He says that in deep thinking, students go beyond the facts and *do something* with those facts. Students move beyond memorization and toward deeper levels of learning and understanding by engaging in cognitive processes that require them to elaborate upon and transform the content into some different form.

Cuseo has developed a classification system to organize a variety of cognitive skills that would be included in his more inclusive definition of critical thinking. This system (which you'll find at the end of his 2000 article) includes the cognitive processes of:

- Comprehension
- Application
- Analysis
- Synthesis
- Evaluation
- Deduction
- Induction
- Adduction (making a case for an argument by accumulating supportive evidence)
- Refutation (accumulating evidence that rebuts a position)
- Balanced thinking
- Multiple perspective taking
- Causal reasoning
- Ethical reasoning
- Creative thinking

Cuseo offers an extensive list of questions we can use to elicit these types of cognitive processing from our students. For comprehension, the question might be as simple as: "How would you put _____ into your own words?" For one aspect of analysis—deconstruction—Cuseo suggests this question: "What assumptions/biases underlie or are hidden within _____?" For the cognitive process of evaluation, he offers this question: "How would you judge the accuracy or validity of _____?" For the process of deduction: "What specific conclusions can be drawn from this general _____?"

Although we've recognized the importance of critical thinking for a couple of decades in the academic world, we've been inconsistent about defining it and developing pedagogies that foster it. More training is needed to help teachers learn how to get students to think beyond learning factual material. We need to learn what questions to ask to promote deeper levels of cognitive processing, and we must understand what teaching strategies will get students engaged beyond rote memorization.

Information literacy and information technology literacy

In their article "Information Literacy as a Liberal Art: Enlightenment Proposals for a New Curriculum," Shapiro and Hughes (1996, 1) pose some interesting questions concerning the meaning of the terms *information literacy* and *information technology literacy*:

> What sort of "information literacy"—an often-used but dangerously ambiguous concept—should we be promoting, and what should it accomplish? Is it merely something that will reduce the number of tech support calls that we have to deal with? Something that will grease the wheels of the information highway? Something that, as defined by representatives of the library community, enables people to be "effective information consumers"?

> Or is it, should it be, something broader, something that enables individuals not only to use information and information technology effectively and adapt to their constant changes but also to think critically about the entire information enterprise and information society? Something more akin to a "liberal art"—knowledge that is part of what it means to be a free person in the present historical context of the dawn of the information age?

I agree that we need to take this broader view of what information literacy and information technology literacy are all about. The K-12 sector is working on helping students develop information technology literacy long before students enter college, but many students still arrive on our campuses deficient in this particular area. *Technology as a Foundation Skill Area: A Journey toward Information Technology Literacy* (Manitoba Education and Training 1998) explains information technology literacy this way (9):

Information technology-literate students are able to:

- Develop knowledge, ability, and responsibility in the use of information technology.

- Acquire, organize, analyze, evaluate, and present information using appropriate information technology.
- Use information technology to expand their range and effectiveness of communication.
- Solve problems, accomplish tasks, and express creativity, both individually and collaboratively, using information technology.
- Understand the role and impact of information technology and apply ethical, responsible, and legal standards in its use.

The knowledge and skills of the information technology-literate student described above builds upon the definition of technology as a foundation skill area and includes the other mutually supportive foundation skill areas of literacy and communication, problem solving, and human relations. It is critical that the use of information technology support development of these skills.

Part of being a critical thinker is having the ability to differentiate credible sources from unreliable ones. Despite our students' "fluency" with the web, many of them don't know the difference between Wikipedia (one of the web's free encyclopedias) and a peer-reviewed, juried scholarly journal. Many colleges and universities are forging working ties between faculty and library staff to find ways to help students develop information literacy and information technology literacy. Information technology literacy, among other broad skills highlighted above, involves the ability to discern the credibility of information gathered by technological means—primarily the use of the Internet. Institutional libraries are creating packets of information on this topic for distribution to the student body. These packets often include tips on how to search for scholarly articles, both in the library and on the Internet. Since most of our students do their research via the Internet, the instructions for this type of searching must be very clear. They should include examples of how to cite information using various styles—such as MLA (Modern Language Association) and APA (American Psychological Association)—from both print and Internet sources.

Knowing that today's students are often less willing to read instructions than they are to "walk through" how to do something, many faculty members are taking their classes to the library, where a staff member does a hands-on tour. If classrooms are wired, faculty members can invite a librarian into class for a demonstration or take their students through the process themselves. In my classes, I provided a handout I created with the help of the library director. (Note: It's included in the Appendix.)

The learner-centered classroom

The best environment for helping our students develop critical thinking skills, build their informational and technological literacy, and become actively engaged and motivated to learn seems to be the learner-centered classroom rather than the teacher- or content-centered classroom.

There has been a research-based paradigm shift during the 1990s and 2000s from the traditional classroom (teacher-centered and content-driven) to the learner-centered classroom (student-centered and process-driven). The shift ties into the learning assessment movement, which is currently a hot topic throughout the nation; when the focus of the classroom shifts from what the teacher is teaching to what the students are learning, we must develop ways to measure student learning outcomes.

The learner-centered classroom involves a systems change. Many years ago, I completed a clinical training program in family therapy. It was an experience that introduced me to systems theory. Systems theory is a part of many disciplines. Applied to families, it means that every family has a way of operating, mostly on automatic pilot. Family members have certain ways of communicating and behaving, and these modes of operation become fixed —even rigid.

The beauty of the theory when it is applied to doing therapy with families is that if any member of the family system changes, the whole system is forced to change. For example, if a daughter always responds to her father in a particular way and then starts to respond differently, her father is forced to change. Now, there are many pieces of good news and bad news about systems theory. One piece of bad news: I have no direct power to change another person's behavior. But the good news is that I have the power to change *myself*; I can change my behavior and how I respond to someone else. More good news and bad news: If I change, I force the other person or persons in the family to change (good news)—but they may not change the way I want them to (bad news). Here's more good news, though: I can always try something new until I get something that's closer to what I really want.

The problem with families is that they get stuck in ruts and they can't even imagine doing anything differently. I was at a conference once where a very brave married couple volunteered to go on stage and re-enact a struggle they had in their relationship. They chose the difficulty they both experienced when the husband traveled on business. The woman described how much she struggled whenever her husband got ready to leave. She shared with the large audience that she always cried. The husband said that when she cried, he felt guilty. But he said he also got angry because he felt he had to go—it was his job—and that he believed his wife *tried* to make him feel guilty. The therapists asked the couple how they might respond differently, but they were stumped. The woman said, "But I always cry; I can't help it." The husband said, "I always feel guilty and angry." The workshop leader then asked volunteers to come up on stage and role play other possible ways to respond. Teams of participants came up one after another, and each had a different scenario. The original couple stood there gaping because they had never considered that they could respond in other ways.

I tell you this story because in my years of teaching, I experienced many classes where I felt stuck to change the dynamic. The classroom, after all, is a dynamic system involving relationships—faculty-student and student-student interactions—that are similar to family connections. When I say that the shift from teacher-centered to learner-centered classrooms involves a systems change, I mean that we have to recognize that the old system uses the formal lecture (in the most extreme case), without interruption from the students. The instructor delivers a body of information to an audience of students, most of whom take notes. As I discussed earlier, the formal or traditional lecture may be the most efficient, cost-effective way to deliver information. But it seems to be the least productive way for students to learn and retain the material and process the information at deeper levels of understanding. The move to a learner-centered classroom, then, will require you as the instructor to make some major changes. Instead of presenting yourself as the sole authority on the content and seeing your job as a delivery system that has to somehow pour the information into passive student receptacles, you must become a facilitator of student learning. First and foremost, you must create a safe, inclusive learning environment so that students feel comfortable participating. In the learner-centered classroom, you must become creative and develop a diverse repertoire of teaching/learning strategies. It becomes your job to develop learning activities that feature student involvement and interaction.

Developing collaborative learning activities is a topic I discuss at great length in *Successful Beginnings for College Teaching* (McGlynn 2001, 88-100). In that same book (81-88), I offer suggestions on leading effective discussions. Suffice it to say here that our students must become active learners, engaged with the material and with each other. The research literature is teeming with supportive evidence that students' engagement with the course material and their classmates is highly correlated with deeper levels of learning, motivation, and persistence, not to mention degree completion.

As the instructor, then, you need to change the classroom dynamic so that your students are more actively involved with the material and with each other. Help students take more responsibility for and control of their learning by teaching them to see the role they play in their own learning. One of my colleagues, for example, asks her students to write their goals for the course at the start of the term, along with the strategies they'll use to achieve those goals. At midterm, she asks her students to assess their progress.

The learner-centered classroom has a much more participatory atmosphere than does the traditional lecture class. Students in the learner-centered classroom communicate more, articulate what the course content means, and draw more sophisticated cognitive connections. Your job: To create the learning activities, promote student participation, guide the whole process, and evaluate learning outcomes as a means of giving your students constructive feedback to improve the learning process.

Student engagement fosters student success

The learner-centered classroom is especially invaluable because it offers a greater likelihood of fostering student engagement. The more students are engaged with the course material and with each other, the more likely they will learn at a deeper level of understanding. They'll also be more apt to retain what they learn, become critical thinkers, and persist until they earn a degree. As I mentioned earlier, such conclusions are fairly indisputable.

Although these findings apply to *all* adult learners, the research on student engagement may be even more important in helping our Millennial students. The Millennials are the most socially connected generation of students. Although there are pros and cons to this phenomenon in terms of the amount of time Millennials spend "communicating" with each other, we need to capitalize on this generation's desire to connect in our teaching practices. Colleges and universities can also contribute to student success by creating welcoming, inclusive institutional environments; setting high expectations for academic performance; and having clear expectations about behavioral decorum.

All the research seems to come together, merging the need for active learning, student engagement, and the learner-centered classroom as the tri-fold keys to student success. Perhaps the best-known student engagement parameters have been outlined by Chickering and Gamson (1987). Their "Seven Principles for Good Practice in Undergraduate Education" still hold up as a model for all of us as college teachers. You can use them as a teaching template and as a vehicle for faculty discussions and professional development:

Seven principles for good practice in undergraduate education

Chickering and Gamson (1987) identified seven principles for good practice in higher education. They are:

1. GOOD PRACTICE ENCOURAGES CONTACTS BETWEEN STUDENTS AND FACULTY.
    Frequent student-faculty contact, in and out of class, is a most important factor in student motivation and involvement. Faculty concern helps students get through rough times and keep on working. Knowing a few faculty members well enhances students' intellectual commitment and encourages them to think about their own values and plans.

2. GOOD PRACTICE DEVELOPS RECIPROCITY AND COOPERATION AMONG STUDENTS.
    Learning is enhanced when it is more like a team effort than a solo race. Good learning, like good work, is collaborative and social, not competitive and isolated. Working with others often increases involvement in learning. Sharing one's ideas and responding to others' improves thinking and deepens understanding.

3. GOOD PRACTICE USES ACTIVE LEARNING TECHNIQUES.
    Learning is not a spectator sport. Students do not learn much just sitting in classes listening to teachers, memorizing prepackaged assignments, and spitting out answers. They must talk about what they are learning, write reflectively about it, relate it to past experiences, and apply it to their daily lives. They must make what they learn part of themselves.

4. GOOD PRACTICE GIVES PROMPT FEEDBACK.
    Knowing what you know and don't know focuses your learning. In getting started, students need help in assessing their existing knowledge and competence. Then, in classes, students need frequent opportunities to perform and receive feedback on their performance. At various points during college, and at its end, students need chances to reflect on what they have learned, what they still need to know, and how they might assess themselves.

5. GOOD PRACTICE EMPHASIZES TIME ON TASK.
    Time plus energy equals learning. Learning to use one's time well is critical for students and professionals alike. Allocating realistic amounts of time means effective learning for students and effective teaching for faculty.

6. GOOD PRACTICE COMMUNICATES HIGH EXPECTA-
    TIONS.
    Expect more and you will get it. High expectations are important
    for everyone—for the poorly prepared, for those unwilling to exert
    themselves, and for the bright and well motivated. Expecting stu-
    dents to perform well becomes a self-fulfilling prophecy.

7. GOOD PRACTICE RESPECTS DIVERSE TALENTS AND
    WAYS OF LEARNING.
    Many roads lead to learning. Different students bring different
    talents and styles to college. Brilliant students in a seminar might
    be all thumbs in a lab or studio; students rich in hands-on experi-
    ence may not do so well with theory. Students need opportunities
    to show their talents and learn in ways that work for them. Then
    they can be pushed to learn in new ways that do not come so easily.

What Chickering and Gamson said twenty years ago still holds credibility today given the last two decades' worth of research. Moreover, their
last "good practice"—respecting diverse talents and ways of learning—may
be even more meaningful as we try to engage the Net Generation in our
classes.

 Knowing our students

Knowing our students' strengths only adds to our effectiveness as
teachers. As Diana and James Oblinger (2005b) suggest, we need to understand the role of our students' technological expertise in their learning.
Oblinger and Oblinger believe that technological expertise may be a more
relevant variable than generational differences when it comes to learning
styles and preferences. In their discussion of the Net Generation (or any college students who have an ease with computers), the Oblingers tell us that
instead of learning information in a linear way—as previous generations
did—today's students leap around thanks to their familiarity with hypertext
on the computer. Hypertext allows them, for example, to click from web site
to web site in a non-linear way. As a result, many Millennials are capable of
piecing together information from a variety of sources. As faculty members,
then, we must teach our students how to determine whether a source of information is actually a credible one.

Oblinger and Oblinger (2005b, 2.5) describe other notable characteristics of the Net Generation. Among them:

  • Their ability to read visual images—they are intuitive visual
    communicators.

- Their visual-spatial skills—perhaps because of their expertise with games, they can integrate the virtual and the physical.
- Their inductive discovery—they learn better by doing than by being told.
- Their "attentional deployment"—they can shift their attention rapidly from one task to another, and they may not pay attention to things that don't interest them.
- Their fast response time—they respond quickly and expect rapid responses in turn.

Some of these strengths have downsides. For example, the techno-savvy generation's ability to read visual images and move between the real and the virtual—which expands their literacy beyond text—may mean that they rely much less on reading. Consequently, their text literacy may be less developed than it was for students in previous generations. On the other hand, the Oblingers note (2005b) that "students on average retain 10 percent of what they read but closer to 30 percent of what they see" (2.14). The old Chinese proverb "a picture is worth a thousand words" may be particularly applicable to the Net Generation.

Similarly, the downside of desire for immediacy and propensity to multitask is that the Millennials may be prone to sacrifice accuracy for speed. Part of our role as teachers, then, must be to encourage our students to continuously check themselves—especially the conclusions they reach as well as the ways they reach those conclusions.

Using the Millennials' strengths
to teach them more effectively

How can we as teachers use the Millennials' natural strengths to teach them more effectively? If we know that most Millennials prefer learning by doing rather than by being "talked to," we need to capitalize on their desire to learn through discovery. Their social connectedness suggests that we can organize educational activities that involve teamwork and interaction with their peers. Oblinger and Oblinger (2005b) also emphasize the Millennials' need to achieve. These students want to know—explicitly—how they can achieve their goals. Often, their goals involve nothing more than earning a good grade; they want to know how to accomplish even that.

It's clear that this generation has a preference for fast-moving, engaging interactions in the classroom. If the class moves too slowly or isn't interesting, Millennials may well tune out. The Oblingers say we may need to encourage these students to stop experiencing and spend more time reflecting.

We can do that in our classes by requiring very short writing assignments during class that give our students the chance to stop *discussing and doing* and start *thinking and focusing.*

Oblinger and Oblinger (2005b) stress that we are all products of our environments. In order for us to become effective teachers, then, we must understand where we come from as well as what has shaped our students. Age (generation) may be less important than exposure to technology. If technology is an imbedded part of our younger students' worlds and the worlds of some older students as well, we must teach in ways that appeal to that technological bent. However, the Oblingers warn, colleges and universities should not assume that more technology is necessarily better. In fact, the Oblingers note, student technology surveys show that most students prefer only a moderate amount of technology in the instructional process.

The Oblingers also stress (2005b) that Millennials appreciate online syllabi, online class readings, and online submission of assignments. Their strong *preference*, however, is face-to-face interaction. Interestingly, older students are more likely to be satisfied with fully web-based courses than are the Millennials. Oblinger and Oblinger (2005b) tell us that for older students, web-based courses offer convenience and flexibility needed for their lives. They're not looking for as much social interaction as are members of the Net Generation.

The Net Generation likes simulations, visualizations, games, and role playing. We can use their social connectedness in positive ways in our classrooms. As Johnson et al. (1991) found and other research supports, there is a connection between student interaction and retention. None of this information is particularly new. The learner-centered classroom, based on learning theory and empirical evidence, has always advocated for student interaction with the course material, each other, and the teacher. So teachers and students—even if they belong to different generations—may not be all that different. Students from every generation have looked to college as a way to interact with both teachers and fellow students.

In Chapter 2, I referred to the gap between Baby Boomers and Millennials that can interfere with the teaching and learning process. Oblinger and Oblinger (2005b) make a similar point when they say that there is often a difference in perspective between college faculty/administrators and their Millennial students. To best serve their students, those at the helm of colleges and universities must discover who their students are beyond the demographics. Learning about students may involve an institutional commitment to having dialogues with students to uncover how best to meet their educational needs.

What seems evident is that today's youngest students have unique preferences for *how* they learn. Oblinger and Oblinger (2005b) tell us that the Net Generation appreciates more graphics and visuals, a rapid pace, and immediate feedback. They also tell us that it isn't the technology per se that these students find engaging; rather, it's the challenge of the learning activity. For these students, team projects will probably work better than individual learning activities. In my own classes, I often used a brief writing activity to help students reflect and focus. I then had them work in either pairs or groups of four to solve problems together or reach consensus on an issue.

Oblinger and Oblinger (2005b, 2.16) put the role of technology in its proper place:

> With the appropriate use of technology, learning can be made more active, social, and learner centered—but the uses of IT are driven by pedagogy, not technology. Educating students is the primary goal of colleges and universities. However, reaching that goal depends on understanding those learners. Only by understanding the Net Generation can colleges and universities create learning environments that optimize their strengths and minimize their weaknesses. Technology has changed the Net Generation, just as it is now changing higher education.

The final word

For those of us teaching in higher education—particularly at community colleges, where age diversity is greatest—we need to create courses that accommodate varying levels of expertise with technology. We must also offer a variety of teaching and learning modes so that we reach and motivate as many students as we can.

In the Appendix that ends this book, I highlight resources that can be useful for ongoing professional development. I also include my handout on searching for legitimate sources of information.

It may be a stretch to expand your teaching repertoire. But as a friend's bumper sticker asks, "When is the last time you did something for the first time?"

Good luck on your teaching journey.

Appendix

Useful Online Resources
for Professional Development

- www.educause.edu
- www.oncourseworkshop.com
- www.insidehighered.com
- www.magnapubs.com
- www.nisod.org/newsletter/hookem_up1.htm#nisodcast
- www.makingyourmark.com
- http://nsse.iub.edu/nsse_2006_annual_report/ docs/nsse_2006_ annual_report.pdf
- www.ccsse.org/publications/ccssesummary2006.pdf

Example of a Handout
for Promoting Information Searches

TO SEARCH FOR RESEARCH TOPICS, JOURNAL ARTICLES, OR INFORMATION:

To find full-text journal articles, you may go to our library or any college library, where you will find a number of different journals in many fields of study. There is usually a list of what journals the library houses at the reference desk; or, in some libraries, they are listed in the online catalog. There are many indexes to choose from. Indexes are a guide to which periodicals to use in finding articles. After selecting a topic, you can use the most recent articles, which are usually listed and alphabetized. College libraries also have back issues of the journals that you see on display. Reference librarians can be helpful in locating what you're researching.

To do electronic searches on the Internet from your home computer, you are NOW ABLE to access MCCC's library databases. In order to search from your home, you must complete a **Remote Access Agreement Form**. This form is available at the Circulation Desk in the MCCC Libraries, or online at www.mccc.edu/students/library/ra.html. You may also e-mail a reference librarian with questions related to your research. Just click on **Ask a Librarian**. E-mail your research questions to: library@mccc.edu.

From the MCCC College Library, or from home, you may use a computer to do research for your classes. Go to the **MCCC Main Page**, point to **Student Services**, and click on **Library**. Then look under **Connect to Electronic Resources** and click on **Search for Journal** Articles. Lots of databases will come up. You may find **EBSCO HOST – Academic Search Premier (VALE)** useful. You would type in a topic, click on full text and peer reviewed, and type in a publication (the name of a psychology journal; many are listed on your syllabus, or you can ask the desk librarian the names of the psychology journals) with dates not before 2000. In addition to EBSCO HOST, you might also find **PsycINFO** useful. If you just click on **PsycINFO**, you will find (most likely) "Abstracts," which are summaries of full-text articles. Copy the complete reference and ask a reference desk librarian if MCCC has the full-text article. If the resource you need is not available in our library, a service is available to you through which resources can be borrowed from one of over 9,000 libraries. This service is free unless you fail to pick up the item ordered, or the lending library charges a fee. Resources are usually received in 7-10 days. Ask any library staff member for a form to use for this service.

The Most Useful Databases for the Purposes of the Paper You Write in Psychology Courses Is PsycARTICLES

PsycARTICLES is a database that includes more than 25,000 full-text articles from 42 journals published by the American Psychological Association and allied organizations. To access these full-text journals, click on **EBSCO Host — All Databases**. Then click on **EBSCO Host Web**. Next, click on the check mark in the box next to **Academic Search Premier**; this removes the check mark, which is what you want to do. Finally, scroll down to the bottom of the page and click on the box next to PsycArticles and begin your search. Follow the prompts on the screen.

Another database, **LexisNexis,** offers access to more full-text articles than any other database offered by the library, but you may not find useable resources here. If you try LexisNexis, click on **LexisNexis Academic Universe**. Once on the next screen, select **News**, the tab marked **Guided News Search** if you want to search general periodicals. You are now on the main search screen. Under the heading **Select a News Category**, click on the down arrow and highlight **Magazines and Journals**. Enter your **search terms (keywords)**, one in each search term box. Move down the page and select, by using the down arrow, the years you want to search. If you want, you can enter the name of a specific journal that you have verified is indexed in this database (ask a librarian if you're not sure). When you're finished, move to the bottom of the page and click on **Search**. Your search results will appear on the next screen. From the college library, with any of the electronic databases, you may choose to e-mail your searches to your e-mail account or print them in the library for 10 cents per page.

Other useful web sites for research:

- www.apa.org/journals
- www.prenhall.com/aronson
- www.socialpsychology.com
- www.worthpublishers.com
- www.apa.org/journals/dev
- www.psychinnovations.com/linkread.htm
- www.psywww.com/resource/bytopic.htm
- www.findarticles.com

Do not give your credit card number to any electronic database such as www.apa.org/journals, since they may charge a fee for allowing you to download an article.

References for Teaching Today's Students

Alexander-Snow, M. 2004. Dynamics of gender, ethnicity, and race in understanding classroom incivility. *New Directions for Teaching and Learning*, Issue 99, 21–31.

Alexander-Snow, M. 2005. Understanding classroom incivility. In *Coping with Classroom Incivilities: Nanny 9-1-1 for the Professor*. Participant Packet 27–35. STARLINK web seminar, October 20. Available at: sites.actx.edu/~pdevelopment/download/packet1020.pdf.

Amada, G. 1999. *Coping with Misconduct in the College Classroom: A Practical Model.* Asheville, NC: College Administration Publications.

Amada, G., S. Jurhee, J.K. Middendorf, M. Poindexter, and S. Koffler. 1999. *Faculty on the Front Lines: Reclaiming Civility in the Classroom.* Video produced by DALLAS Teleconferences, DALLAS TeleLearning, LeCroy Center for Educational Telecommunications, and the Dallas County Community College District. Taped from April 8 teleconference. Alexandria, VA: PBS Adult Learning Satellite Service.

Anderson, E.L. 2003. Changing U.S. demographics and American higher education. *New Directions for Higher Education*, Issue 121, 3–12.

Angelo, T.A., and K.P. Cross. 1993. *Classroom Assessment Techniques: A Handbook for College Teachers.* San Francisco: Jossey-Bass.

Arenson, K.W. 2006. A decline in foreign students is reversed. *The New York Times*, November 13, A20.

Arnold, R.E. 2004. Demographics and issues of retention. *Black Issues in Higher Education* 21(18): 47.

Asch, S.E. 1951. Effects of group pressure upon the modification and distortion of judgment. In H. Guetzkow (ed.), *Groups, Leadership, and Men.* Pittsburgh, PA: Carnegie Press.

Bank, B.J., R.L. Slavings, and B.J. Biddle. 1990. Effects of peer, faculty, and parental influences on students' persistence. *Sociology of Education* 63(3): 208–225.

BBC News. 2006. Net students "think copying ok." June 18. Available at: news.bbc.co.uk/2/hi/uk_news/education/5093286.stm.

Boice, R. 1996. Classroom incivilities. *Research in Higher Education* 37(4): 453–486.

Bonwell, C.C., and J.A. Eison. 1991. *Active Learning: Creating Excitement in the Classroom*. San Francisco: Jossey-Bass.

Briggs, T.W., and A. Gonzalez. 2006. Josephson Institute's 2006 report card on the ethics of American youth. *USA Today* Snapshots, December 13, 1.

Brown, J.S. 2000. Growing up digital: How the web changes work, education, and the ways people learn. *Change: The Magazine of Higher Learning* 32(2):10–20.

Brown, M. 2005. Learning spaces. In D.G. Oblinger and J.L. Oblinger (eds.), *Educating the Net Generation*. Boulder, CO: EDUCAUSE. Available at: www.educause.edu/educatingthenetgen.

Burns, M.U. 1999. All the world's a stage. *NEA Higher Education Advocate*, October, 5–8.

Chickering, A.W., and Z.F. Gamson. 1987. Seven principles for good practice in undergraduate education. *AAHE Bulletin* 39(7): 3–7.

Chismark, S., L. Duvall, and M. Alexander-Snow. 2005. *Coping with Classroom Incivilities: Nanny 9-1-1 for the Professor*. STARLINK web seminar, October 20. Available at: sites.actx.edu/~pdevelopment/download/packet1020.pdf.

Clavner, J. 2006. Telephones and the professor. *NISOD Innovation Abstracts* 28(18): 2.

Community College Survey of Student Engagement. 2005. *Engaging Students, Challenging the Odds: 2005 Findings*. Available at: www.ccsse.org/publications/CCSSE_reportfinal2005.pdf.

Community College Survey of Student Engagement. 2006. Executive Summary: *Act on Fact: Using Data to Improve Student Success*. Available at: www.ccsse.org/publications/CCSSESummary2006.pdf.

Cuseo, J. 2000. Questions that promote deeper thinking. Available at: oncourseworkshop.com/Learning030.htm.

DeBarros, A. 2003. New baby boom swamps colleges. *USA Today*, January 2, A1–A2.

Dewey, J. 1963. *Experience and Education*. New York: Collier Books.

Diener, E., R. Lusk, D. DeFour, and R. Flax. 1980. Deindividuation: Effects of group size, density, number of observers, and group member similarity on self-consciousness and disinhibited behavior. *Journal of Personality and Social Psychology* 39(3): 449–459.

Eckholm, E. 2006. Plight deepens for black men, studies warn. *The New York Times*, March 20, A1.

Edelman, P., H.J. Holzer, and P. Offner. 2006. *Reconnecting Disadvantaged Young Men*. Washington, DC: Urban Institute Press.

Elliott, J. 2003–2006. "Jane Elliott's Blue Eyes/Brown Eyes Exercise" web site. Available at: www.janeelliott.com.

Epstein, D. 2006. Be polite, e-polite. *Inside Higher Education*, April 19. Available at: www.insidehighered.com/news/2006/04/19/oregon.

Ewers, J. 2002. Get to work. *U.S. News & World Report*, April 29, 44.

Foreman, J. 2003. Next-generation educational technology versus the lecture. *EDUCAUSE Review* 38(4): 12–22.

Fortney, S.D., D.I. Johnson, and K.M. Long. 2001. The impact of compulsive communicators on the self-perceived competence of classroom peers: An investigation and test of instructional strategies. *Communication Education* 50(4): 357–373.

Frand, J.L. 2000. The Information-Age mindset: Changes in students and implications for higher education. *EDUCAUSE Review* 35(5): 14–24.

Frost, W.L. 1999–2000. It takes a community to retain a student: The Trinity Law School Model. *Journal of College Student Retention* 1(3): 203–223.

Fry, R. 2002. *Latinos in Higher Education: Many Enroll, Too Few Graduate*. Washington, DC: The Pew Hispanic Center.

Gallant, T.B., and P. Drinan. 2006. Organizational theory and student cheating: Explanation, responses, and strategies. *Journal of Higher Education* 77(5): 839–860.

Gerald, D.E., and W.J. Hussar. 2002. *Projections of Education Statistics to 2012*. Washington, DC: U.S. Department of Education, National Center for Education Statistics. Publication NCES 2002-030. Available at: nces.ed.gov/pubs2002/2002030.pdf.

Giegerich, S. 2004. Report: Colleges not ready for influx of Hispanics. *USA Today*, February 3.

Hakimzadeh, S. 2006. *41.9 Million and Counting: A Statistical View of Hispanics at Mid-Decade*. Washington, DC: Pew Research Center. Available at: pewresearch.org/pubs/251/419-million-and-counting.

Halperin, S. 2006. Comments on *Reconnecting Disadvantaged Young Men*. See: www.urban.org/pubs/reconnecting/ecomments.html.

Halstead, N., and J. Tomson. Unpublished. *Critical Thinking: ETS Project for June 2006*.

Hamm, R.E. 2004. *Going to College: Not What It Used to Be. Keeping America's Promise. A Joint Publication of the Education Commission of the States and the League for Innovation in the Community College*. Denver, CO: Education Commission of the States.

Hansen, E.J. 1998. Essential demographics of today's college students. *AAHE Bulletin* 51(3): 3–5.

Howe, N., and W. Strauss. 2000. *Millennials Rising: The Next Great Generation*. New York: Vintage Books.

Houston, L. 2007. Brown bag introductions. Available at: www.oncourseworkshop.com/Getting%20On%20Course005.htm.

Jayson, S. 2006. Are social norms steadily unraveling? *USA Today*, April 13, D4.

Johnson, D.W., R.T. Johnson, and K.A. Smith. 1991. *Cooperative Learning: Increasing College Faculty Instructional Productivity*. ASHE-ERIC Higher Education Report No. 4. Washington, DC: George Washington University School of Education and Human Development.

Johnson, E. 1999. Preclude cheating: A response. *The Teaching Professor*, August/September, 5.

Kuh, G.D., J. Kinzie, J.H. Schuh, E.J. Whitt, and Associates. 2005. *Student Success in College: Creating Conditions That Matter*. San Francisco: Jossey-Bass.

Lash, J. 2004. Number of high school graduates expected to rise. *Scripps Howard Foundation Wire*, January 29.

Malveaux, J. 2006. Minority college aid suffers from attacks. *USA Today*, March 17, A13.

Manitoba Education and Training. 1998. *Technology as a Foundation Skill Area: A Journey toward Information Technology Literacy*. Winnipeg: Manitoba Education and Training. Available at: www.edu.gov.mb.ca/k12/docs/support/tfs/pdfed_tech.pdf.

Manning, T.M., B. Everett, and C. Roberts. 2006. *The Millennial Generation: The Next Generation in College Enrollment*. STARLINK web seminar, February 4. Available at: www.cpcc.edu/planning. (Click on "Studies and Reports" and then "Full Millennial Generation Presentation.")

McCabe, D.L. (Interview). 2000. New research on academic integrity: The success of "modified" honor codes. *Synfax Weekly Report*, May 15, 975. Available at: www.collegepubs.com/ref/SFX000515.shtml.

McCabe, D.L., and L.K. Trevino. 1996. What we know about cheating in college: Longitudinal trends and recent developments. *Change: The Magazine of Higher Learning* 28(1): 28–32.

McGlynn, A.P. 2000. The changing face of the student body: The challenges before us. *Hispanic Outlook in Higher Education* 11(1): 33–34.

McGlynn, A.P. 2001. *Successful Beginnings for College Teaching: Engaging Your Students from the First Day*. Madison, WI: Atwood Publishing.

McGlynn, A.P. 2004a. Projected demographics a wake-up call for academia. *Hispanic Outlook in Higher Education* 15(1): 34–35.

McGlynn, A.P. 2004b. Ph.D.s look at the community college: Perspectives from Mercer County and Shoreline Community College. *Hispanic Outlook in Higher Education* 14(19): 18–20.

McGlynn, A.P. 2005. Teaching millennials: Greater need for student-centered learning. *Hispanic Outlook in Higher Education* 16(1): 19–20.

McGlynn, A.P. 2006a. LISTO assures transfer success at College of the Sequoias. *Hispanic Outlook in Higher Education* 16(25): 30.

McGlynn, A.P. 2006b. The worsening plight of black men. *Hispanic Outlook in Higher Education* 17(3): 17–18.

Mehaffy, G. (Moderator), and D.G. Oblinger. 2005. *Listening to What We're Seeing: Generational Styles and Learning Characteristics.* Society for College and University Planning and American Association of State Colleges and Universities web seminar, November 17, 2005. Available at: www.scup.org/profdev/archive_cds/lwws.html.

Mincy, R.B. 2006. *Black Males Left Behind.* Washington, DC: Urban Institute Press.

Moore, A.H., J.F. Moore, and S.B. Fowler. 2005. Faculty development for the Net Generation. In D.G. Oblinger and J.L. Oblinger (eds.), *Educating the Net Generation.* Boulder, CO: EDUCAUSE. Available at: www.educause.edu/educatingthenetgen.

Munde, D. 2002. Three-Point Oral Communication Check-Up. *Mercer County Community College* 3(6): 1.

Nathan, R. 2005. *My Freshman Year: What a Professor Learned by Becoming a Student.* Ithaca, NY: Cornell University Press.

National Survey of Student Engagement. 2005. *Exploring Different Dimensions of Student Engagement: 2005 Annual Survey Results.* Available at: nsse.iub.edu/pdf/NSSE2005_annual_report.pdf.

Noel-Levitz. 2007. *National Freshman Attitudes Report.* Iowa City, IA: Noel-Levitz. Available at: www.noellevitz.com.

Oblinger, D. 2003. Boomers, Gen-Xers, & Millennials: Understanding the new students. *EDUCAUSE Review* 38(4): 37–47.

Oblinger, D.G. 2005. Learners, learning, & technology: The EDUCAUSE Learning Initiative. *EDUCAUSE Review* 40(5): 66–75.

Oblinger, D.G., and B.L. Hawkins. 2005. IT myths: The myths about students. *EDUCAUSE Review* 40(5): 12–13.

Oblinger, D.G., and J.L. Oblinger (eds.). 2005a. *Educating the Net Generation*. Boulder, CO: EDUCAUSE. Available at: www.educause.edu/educatingthenetgen.

Oblinger, D.G., and J.L. Oblinger. 2005b. Is it age or IT: First steps toward understanding the Net Generation. In D.G. Oblinger and J.L. Oblinger (eds.), *Educating the Net Generation*. Boulder, CO: EDUCAUSE. Available at: www.educause.edu/educatingthenetgen.

Orfield, G. 2004. *Dropouts in America: Confronting the Graduation Rate Crisis*. Cambridge, MA: Harvard Education Press.

Padilla, R.V. 1999. College student retention: Focus on success. *Journal of College Student Retention* 1(2): 131–145.

Patterson, O. 2006. A poverty of the mind. *The New York Times*, March 26, 4.13.

Paul, R., and L. Elder. 2002. *A Miniature Guide for Those Who Teach on How to Improve Student Learning: 30 Practical Ideas*. Dillon Beach, CA: Foundation for Critical Thinking.

Paul, R., and L. Elder. 2006. *The Miniature Guide to Critical Thinking: Concepts and Tools*. Dillon Beach, CA: Foundation for Critical Thinking.

Piaget, J. 1952. *The Origins of Intelligence in Children*, M. Cook (trans.). New York: International Universities Press.

Prensky, M. 2001. Digital Natives, Digital Immigrants. *On the Horizon* 9(5): 1–6.

Prentice-Dunn, S., and R.W. Rogers. 1989. Deindividuation and the self-regulation of behavior. In P.B. Paulus (ed.), *The Psychology of Group Influence*. Hillsdale, NJ: Lawrence Erlbaum Associates.

President's Advisory Commission on Educational Excellence for Hispanic Americans. 1996. *Our Nation on the Fault Line: Hispanic American Education*. Washington, DC: U.S. Department of Education.

Pulley, J.L. 2006. Crossing borders. *Community College Week* 19(3): 6–9.

Raines, C. 2002. Managing millennials. Available at: www.generationsatwork.com/articles/millenials.htm.

Reesor, L., and K. Schlabach. 2006. Managing multi-generations: Strategies for crossing the generational divide in the workplace. *Leadership Exchange* 4(3): 16.

Richardson, R.C., Jr., and A.G. de los Santos, Jr. 1988. *Helping Minority Students Graduate from College: A Comprehensive Approach*. Washington, DC: ERIC Clearinghouse on Higher Education. Publication ED308795.

Richardson, S.M. (ed.). 1999. *Promoting Civility: A Teaching Challenge*. New Directions for Teaching and Learning, Issue 77. San Francisco: Jossey-Bass.

Richardson, S.M. 2000. Civility: What went wrong? *NEA Higher Education Advocate* 17(5): 5–7.

Rooney, P., and T.D. Snyder (eds.). 2006. *The Condition of Education 2006.* Washington, DC: U.S. Department of Education, National Center for Education Statistics. Publication NCES 2006-071. Available at: nces.ed.gov/pubsearch/pubsinfo.asp?pubid=2006071.

Rosenthal, N. 1990. Active learning/empowered learning. *Adult Learning* 1(5): 16–18.

Rosenthal, R., and L. Jacobson. 1968. *Pygmalion in the Classroom.* New York: Holt, Rinehart & Winston.

Sacks, P. 1996. *Generation X Goes to College: An Eye-Opening Account of Teaching in Postmodern America.* Peru, IL: Open Court.

Schneider, A. 1998. Insubordination and intimidation signal the end of decorum in many classrooms. *The Chronicle of Higher Education*, March 27, A12–A14.

Senge, P. 1990. The leader's new work: Building learning organizations. *Sloan Management Review* 32(1): 7–23.

Shapiro, J.J., and S.K. Hughes. 1996. Information literacy as a liberal art: Enlightenment proposals for a new curriculum. *EDUCOM Review* 31(2): 31–35.

Silberman, M. 1996. *Active Learning: 101 Strategies to Teach Any Subject.* Needham Heights, MA: Allyn and Bacon.

Skiba, D.J., and A.J. Barton. 2006. Adapting your teaching to accommodate the Net Generation of learners. *Online Journal of Issues in Nursing* 11(2). Available at: www.nursingworld.org/ojin/topic30/tpc30_4.htm.

Snyder, T.D., A.G. Tan, and C.M. Hoffman. 2006. *Digest of Education Statistics, 2005.* Washington, DC: U.S. Department of Education, National Center for Education Statistics. Publication NCES 2006-030. Available at: nces.ed.gov/pubsearch/pubsinfo.asp?pubid=2006030.

Sweeney, R. (Moderator) and Students. 2006. *The Millennial Generation.* Distance Learning Academic Advisory Board (DLAAB) Faculty Colloquium, NJEDge.Net, New Jersey Institute of Technology, February 17. PowerPoint available at: www.library.njit.edu/staff-folders/sweeney.

Tavris, C., and E. Aronson. 2003. *Cooperation, Compassion, and Civility in the Classroom.* STARLINK web seminar, February 17.

Turner, R.C. 1999. Adapting to a new generation of college students. *Thought & Action* 15(2): 33–41.

The Urban Institute (News Release). 2006. New approaches address getting alienated young men back to school or jobs. January 12. Available at: www.urban.org/publications/900909.html.

Twenge, J. 2006. *Generation Me: Why Today's Young Americans Are More Confident, Assertive, Entitled—and More Miserable Than Ever Before.* New York: Free Press.

VanSlyke, T. 2003. Digital Natives, Digital Immigrants: Some thoughts from the generation gap. *The Technology Source*, May/June. Available at: technology source.org/article/digital_natives_digital_immigrants.

Wallis, C., W. Cole, S. Steptoe, and S.S. Dale. 2006. The multitasking generation. *Time*, March 27, 48–55.

Weimer, M. 2002. *Learner-Centered Teaching: Five Key Changes to Practice*. San Francisco: Jossey-Bass.

Western Interstate Commission for Higher Education. 2003. *Knocking at the College Door: Projections of High School Graduates by State, Income, and Race/Ethnicity*. Boulder, CO: Western Interstate Commission for Higher Education.

Western Interstate Commission for Higher Education (News Release). 2004. The Class of 2008, and Beyond: New study projects more graduates and greater diversity at the nation's high schools, with dramatic differences between states and regions. January 29. Available at: www.wiche.edu/policy/knocking/press_release.pdf.

Wilgoren, J. 2000. Swell of minority students is predicted at colleges. *The New York Times*, May 24, A16.

Williamson, C. 2002. The war of the ages. *Planning* 68(7): 4–9.

Wilson, C.D. 2004. Coming through the open door: A student profile. In K. Boswell and C.D. Wilson (eds.), *Keeping America's Promise: A Report on the Future of the Community College. A joint publication of Education Commission of the States and League for Innovation in the Community College*. Denver, CO: Education Commission of the States.

Wilson, J.L. 1998. Generation X: Who are they? What do they want? *Thought & Action* 14(2): 9–18.

Wirt, J., and T.D. Snyder (eds.). 2002. *The Condition of Education 2002*. Washington, DC: U.S. Department of Education, National Center for Education Statistics. Publication NCES 2002-025. Available at: nces.ed.gov/pubsearch/pubsinfo.asp?pubid=2002025.

Zernike, K. 2006. College, my way. *The New York Times*, Education Life Supplement, April 23, 24–28.

Zimbardo, P.G. 1970. The human choice: Individuation, reason, and order versus deindividuation, impulse, and chaos. In W.J. Arnold and D. Levine (eds.), *1969 Nebraska Symposium on Motivation*. Lincoln: University of Nebraska Press.

About the Author

Angela Provitera McGlynn is a retired Professor of Psychology at Mercer County Community College in West Windsor, New Jersey, where she taught more than 13,000 students over a career spanning 35 years. She is the author of *Successful Beginnings for College Teaching: Engaging Your Students from the First Day* (Atwood Publishing, 2001) as well as three other books on college teaching. She has also written numerous journal articles, presented workshops across the United States, and appeared on radio and national television programs.